SACRED VOWS

អធិដ្ឋានពិសិដ្ឋ

Vat Ek, Battambang. Cambodia. Sandstone 1002–1050.

Sacred Vows

POETRY BY U SAM OEUR

TRANSLATED FROM KHMER BY
KEN McCULLOUGH AND U SAM OEUR

COFFEE HOUSE PRESS ☕ MINNEAPOLIS

These poems have appeared in the following magazines and periodicals: *The Iowa Alumni Review; Exchanges: A Journal of Translation; 100 Words; Nebraska Humanities; Artful Dodge; Green Fuse; Manoa; Briar Cliff Review; The Iowa Review; Earth's Daughters: A Feminist Periodical; Modern Poetry in Translation; Muse News for S.O.M.O.S.; Press; Cambodian Network Council; Asian Pages; Journal of the Asian American Renaissance.* Twelve of the poems appeared in a special issue of *No Exit.* "Exodus," "The Loss of My Twins" and "The Krasang Tree at Prek Po" were reprinted in the anthology *Voices of Conscience: Poetry from Oppression,* Iron Press, Manchester, England. Nine of the poems appeared in an en face (Khmer and English) chapbook entitled *Selections from Sacred Vows,* Zephyr Limited Editions Chapbook Series.

Coffee House Press is supported in part by a grant provided by the Minnesota State Arts Board, through an appropriation by the Minnesota State Legislature, and in part by a grant from the National Endowment for the Arts. Significant support has also been provided by the McKnight Foundation; Lannan Foundation; Jerome Foundation; Target Stores, Dayton's, and Mervyn's by the Dayton Hudson Foundation; General Mills Foundation; The St. Paul Companies; Butler Family Foundation; Honeywell Foundation; Star Tribune/Cowles Media Company; Beverly J. and John A. Rollwagen Fund of the Minneapolis Foundation; James R. Thorpe Foundation; Dain Bosworth Foundation; Pentair, Inc.; the Helen L. Kuehn Fund of the Minneapolis Foundation; the Peter & Madeleine Martin Fundation; the law firm of Schwegman, Lundberg, Woessner & Kluth, P.A.; and many individual donors. To you and our many readers across the country, we send our thanks for your continuing support.

Coffee House Press books are available to the trade through our primary distributor, Consortium Book Sales & Distribution, 1045 Westgate Drive, Saint Paul, MN 55114. For personal orders, catalogs, or other information, write to: Coffee House Press, 27 N. 4th Street, Suite 400, Minneapolis, MN 55401.

LIBRARY OF CONGRESS CIP DATA
U Sam Oeur, 1936 –
   Sacred Vows : poems / by U Sam Oeur ; translated from Khmer by Ken McCullough and U Sam Oeur.
     p. cm.
   ISBN 1-56689-069-1 (pbk. : alk. paper)
   I. Cambodia—Poetry. 2. Liberty—Poetry. I. McCullough, Ken. II. Title.
   PL4328.9.U16S231998
   895.932—dc21   97-43267
                                                 CIP

10 9 8 7 6 5 4 3 2 1
first edition / first printing
printed in Canada

CONTENTS

TRANSLATOR'S INTRODUCTION

In a century which continues to be pockmarked with horrific episodes of genocide and "ethnic cleansing," the Pol Pot regime in Cambodia stands out as being particularly egregious; approximately 1.5 million Cambodians (out of a total of 7.9 million) perished from disease, starvation, exhaustion, or were executed from early 1975 through early 1979, when the Vietnamese "liberated" Cambodia from the Khmer Rouge. In Cambodia, it was mostly Cambodians killing off Cambodians essentially indistinguishable from themselves, but the regime was particularly hard on the Vietnamese, Cham (Islamic Khmer), and Chinese communities in Cambodia. In Marxist-Leninist terms, it was a class war in which anyone tainted by foreign influence, particularly in terms of education and/or capitalist ideology, was considered "the enemy," although, ironically, the perpetrators themselves had been educated in France. From the start, teachers, doctors, and those who had served in the military were executed, but after 1977 the definition of "the enemy" veered uncontrollably from week to week, and internal purges occurred on a regular basis.

U Sam Oeur is a survivor of the Pol Pot regime and the ensuing period under Vietnamese control. This volume of poems presents his eyewitness account of those experiences. He was born in 1936 in rural Svey Rieng province, into the large family of a relatively prosperous farmer. Sam, as he is known to his friends, spent most of his early life engaged in the daily routine of planting and harvesting rice and tending the water buffalo herd. Sam had older brothers who were educated, and he eventually followed suit.

In 1962, he was selected to attend Cal State/Los Angeles to pursue a degree in the teaching of industrial arts. While he was a student there, Mary Gray, the executive director of the Asia Foundation, discovered some of Sam's random jottings and told him that he was an accomplished poet, which was news to Sam, since he had no idea what poetry was. Nonetheless, Mary Gray arranged for Sam to enroll in the MFA program at the University of Iowa's Writers Workshop. I entered the MFA program that same year, and Sam and I became neighbors and close friends.

Sam completed his studies in 1968, returned to Cambodia, married, and assumed a succession of roles in Cambodian light industry. He was also elected to Parliament and was chosen as a member of a delegation to the U.N. and served two years in the military. We corresponded for a while but Sam told me that all the mail was being censored; hence, there was little point in writing anymore. Then came April 17, 1975. Sam and his family and the rest of the 1.8 million occupants of Phnom Penh were driven out of the city by the Khmer Rouge. During the next four years Sam lost many of his relatives, including the twin girls his wife gave birth to. But Sam, his wife, son, and mother-in-law survived life in six different concentration camps. Sam himself avoided being recognized as an intellectual by feigning illiteracy and by resorting to knowledge gained during his childhood on the farm—this despite elaborate ploys by the camp officials to trick him into revealing his true identity.

After "liberation," Sam reentered the workforce and eventually became the Assistant Minister of Industry, until a pro-democracy poem was discovered in his office desk. The party forced him to sign a letter of resignation from his position and he became persona non grata and a target of continued harassment. Incidentally, he has continued to receive death threats here in the U.S.

Upon learning in 1984 that Sam was still alive, I resumed a correspondence with him through an Australian nongovernmental organization in Thailand and approached Clark Blaise, director of the University of Iowa's International Writing Program, about getting Sam out of Cambodia to visit the U.S. Clark was definitely interested but had problems getting backing for Sam, since Sam was not a well-established writer. Of course, had he been well established, he would have been one of the first to be exterminated under Pol Pot. Sam had, in fact, destroyed his copy of his MFA thesis along with an eighty-page poetry manuscript. After much finagling, Clark arranged for Sam to be a participant in the program. When I met Sam at the airport in September 1992 he had a small suitcase full of tattered reference books and a few scraps of notes—the rest of his work was in his head. We immediately began the arduous task of getting this material down on paper, since we did not know if we could get his visa extended beyond January. Sam did receive an extension and has since applied for political asylum. Sam lives in Minneapolis, and his son and daughter-in-law (and grandson) live in Dallas. Sam's wife has chosen to remain in Phnom Penh to care for her aging mother.

❈ ❈

Traditional Cambodian poetry includes forty-six set forms, although most poets rarely use more than the same five or six. Poetry is traditionally chanted in a monotone, but U Sam Oeur's style is distinct in that it has operatic qualities—narrative passages are chanted in a conversational tone, but passages which revolve around loss (and are addressed to an individual) are delivered in a manner comparable to the most emotionally charged aria. It is difficult to capture the spirit of U Sam Oeur's poetry in English and impossible to render the manner in which he chants it, short of including a cassette or musical score with the text. Some of these translations are literal, others work toward capturing the spirit of the poems rather than the exact words.

Khmer poetry is usually steeped in references to the golden age of Cambodian culture, the Angkor era, which lasted from the 10th to the 14th century and borrows heavily from the myths of Indian tradition. When spiritual matters are broached, one will often find Pali words infiltrating the poetry, as Pali is the language appropriate to such subjects, much as Sanskrit would be to Hindi poets. Most polysyllabic words in Khmer have been appropriated from other languages.

U Sam Oeur's poetry adheres to traditional forms in most cases, but now and then he will write in free verse, which does not exist in Cambodian tradition. And his poetry uses the myths, stories, and prophecies of tradition as ironic counterpoint to Cambodia's present-day situation. It is Sam's hope that he will begin to nudge Cambodian people out of living in the Angkor era into a present which is tempered by traditions but not encumbered by them. We are, for instance, in the midst of translating Whitman's "Song of Myself" into Khmer, and it is Sam's hope to someday open a creative writing school in Cambodia, for Cambodians as well as people from other countries. Younger Cambodians born here in the u.s. are often as cut off from Cambodian culture as they would have been during the Pol Pot regime. It is our hope that this volume will inspire them to immerse themselves in their heritage and make those traditions once again vibrant living entities.

❧ ❧

Many people (and organizations) have helped keep Sam afloat physically, emotionally, and spiritually since his arrival here in the u.s. This list includes Mary Gray (his mentor), Clark Blaise, Voha Chuon (of the Voice of America) and Nakry Chuon, Sam Ang Sam, Carol Harke, Marlene Perrin, Maggie Hogan, Cynthia Bishara, Rowena Torrevillas, April McAllister, Gregory Ann Smith, Mom Ven, Luckchhman Kim, the Lillian Hellman-Dashiell Hammett Fund for Free Expression, P.E.N., the St. Paul Companies, Ginny and Mike Duncan, the congregation of the First Mennonite Church of Iowa City (especially Pastor Firman Gingerich and Hobart Yoder), St. Anthony's Bread (of St. Mary's Roman Catholic Church of Iowa City, administered by Adelaide Bulgarelli), the Martin Foundation of New Mexico, the members of the Society of the Muse of the Southwest, the people of Taos (especially Mag Dimond, Charlie Strong, Rose Rutherford, Lorraine Ciancio, Steve Rose, Sy and Phyllis Hotch), Ed Folsom, Dannie Weissbort, Ray Heffner, Julie Englander, Michael Dennis Browne, the United Cambodian Association of Minnesota (especially Katherine Cohen and Nancy J. Hall), Mark Bruckner and Mary Beth Easley and the cast of "Krasang Tree," Mr. and Mrs. Meas Koy Kim, Samreth Kim and Vuthy Phok Kim, Noeung Ourn, Khu Kim Touy, Sarem Neou, Kim Son, a host of editors who have been receptive to Sam's poetry, and the individuals at universities and colleges who have sponsored Sam's recitations of his work.

—Ken McCullough
Winona, Minnesota
August 1996

For my Benefactress
Mary F. Gray

Part 1

※ ※

Prophecies & Études

គន្ធទំនាយ ភាគ ១

ផ្ទរលាន់ទិសបូព៌ិស្សូរក្រេដុក
កំពុសឡើងពងលើកំពូលភ្នំ

អ្នកតាចាស់ស្រុកឆោabdៃយំ
កុក ស សំឃិក្នុងគុម្ពក្រែង ។

ពោធិព្រឹក្សចាប់លាស់អត់ចាក់ប្ួស
ក្របីលាក់ខ្លួនព្ទូនសំរួចស្មែង

ពស់វែកមានព៌សដំកន្ទែង
រាជហង្សហើរស្មែងកាច់សំបុក ។

ពពេចក្រាបពងក្រោមគគ្ខា
អ្នកផងយឺ៊ញហើយខំរីសទុក

ភ្លែកពាំផ្លេល្ងរាយគ្រប់ស្រុក
គំណទោមុខទេបជឹងខ្ទន ។

កុក ស កវែងឯកអ្នកខ្ទូ

ថាជឹងចំន្ទុត្រីក្នុងទឹក ។

កុកសាប់រកស៊ុំដោយវាលត្រាញ
ទោះសីហនាទគតាគនឹក

សស្រាក់សស្រាញ់គ្ខូនចាប់ភ្លុក
ចាប់ត្រីទល់ព្រឹកគតមេគ្ខា ។

ខ្លាញ់រកស៊ុំដោយសមសាន្ត
លុះដល់ផ្ទរលាន់គ្រប់ទិសា

លាក់ខ្លួនសម្រាន្តចាំសាសនា
ទេបខ្លាយាត្រាលត់ភ្លឺងព្រៃ ។

រឹងគោស្រុកនិងកុក ស
ហាក់ដូចជាមិត្តស្ទិនស្នេហា

សព្ទថ្ងៃអបរស្រឡាញ់គ្ខា
តែថាគំនិតចិត្តទីទៃ ។

INTDA'S PROPHECY 1

Thunder in the East makes the sound *traDOK!*
the local elders cross their arms and cry
while crayfish crawl to the mountaintop to spawn
and the white egrets stay concealed in the reeds.

The bodhi tree gives leaf though it has no roots
the cobra builds up its venom by staying coiled in its den,
buffalo hide themselves to hone their horns
while the king of swans flies in search of a nest site.

Popich incubate their eggs underwater
while blackcrows carry off figs to disseminate over the land.
Everyone picks them up and stores them.
Later, they will know that they were wrong for doing so.

The long-necked white egrets brag
that they know the number of fish in the water,

while the gray egrets are looking for food in the marshes,
enjoying their lives unobtrusively.
Even though Sieha walks about with fierce bearing,
they continue to glut themselves until dawn.

The she-tiger makes a living in her jungle refuge,
hiding herself for an appropriate time,
and when thunder rumbles in every quarter,
she will leave her sanctuary to squelch the wildfire.

Though domestic bulls and white egrets
appear to show love for each other nowadays,
as if they are intimate friends,
their thoughts are, in fact, duplicitous.

ឯកុតនិងខ្លានៅដោយខ្លួន   ពុំបានជួបជួនគ្នាឡើយនៃ
តែជួបកាលណាអស្ចារ្យបីក្រ   គ្រប់សាសន៍ដៃទេភ័យមិនខាន ។

ព្រោះអ្នកទាំងពីរសិងកាច។   សិងមានអំណាចគ្រប់។ប្រាណ
មានឫទ្ធិអានុភាពពន់ប្រមាណ   ហើយខ្លាំងក្យាហានឥតឧបមា ។

ឥឡូវយើងសូរអ្នកទាំងឡ្យាយ   តើអ្នករុមកាយចូលខាងណា
អ្នកចូលខាងកុកឬខាងខ្យ   អ្នកមានប្រាជ្ញាទើបចូលត្រូវ ។

On the other hand, egrets and tigers stay separate;
they never meet each other.
Once they *do* come up against each other
every nation will shudder,

for these two beasts are ferocious;
they practice strategies, tactics, and tricks;
both of them are powerful,
mightier than thunderbolts.

Now we ask you to stand and be counted—
which side are you on?
Are you for the egrets, or are you pro-tiger?
Only those with vision can make the right choice.

តន្ទុទំនាយ ភាគ ២

មុខគូរស្រណោះនគរគោកធ្លក
តឡូវស្ងាត់រលីឬ្បាងបី

ពីដើមរឿងមកឥតដែលឆ្លើ
អ្នកស្រុកប្រុសស្រីស្ងួដើមឯង ។

ពានរចាប់កូនជ្ជនសត្តខ្លា
មិនមានអាណិតគិតកូនព្រាង

ស៊ីជាអាហារសប្បាយលេង
ហេតុតែវឆ្លេងភ្លេចវិញ្ញាណ ។

អុះឱ អាសូររាជសីសត្ត
មិនឃើញអ្នកមកចែងទទ្លាន

ម្លេចទ្លើយជ្រកបាត់ក្នុងហោមពាន្ត
ឬអាក់អន់អៀនដំណើរអ្វី ។

ឬម្ងួយអ្នកឃើញប៉ិងហេងហ្លួត
ឬឃើញស្ងាត់រលីឬ្បាងបី

ពិរុណារីងសួតវិនាសត្រី
ទើបបានជាថ្ងៃមិនចេញមក ។

បាត់សួ្យយ៉ាងហ្ញឹងដឹងយ៉ាងណា
ឬម្ងួយគ្មានម្ងប់នឹងណប់ជ្រក

ឬចាំអាចារ្យទៅតាមរក
ទើបកែវពន្ធកមិនមកអាយ ។

ម្លេចអ្នកក៏មិនអាសូរសត្ត
សព្ទថ្ងៃគ្មានសោះហោសប្បាយ

រងកម្មពោកក្ដាត់លំបាកកាយ
ព្រាយឈ្មោស់នៀយឈ្មោយឥតឧបមា ។

គ្មិតស្រុកតឡូវុខុសសណ្ណាប់
មច្ឆាខ្លាចប៉ឹង អ្នកដឹងទេ

ក្រពើលង់ស្ងាប់ក្នុងទន្លេ
កូនខ្លាខ្លាចមេ ភ័ខ្លាចត្រី ។

INTDA'S PROPHECY 2

Take pity on Nokor Kok Thlok—
in the old days, we had a life without worries,
now, two shoulders carry three stocks,
and the locals are forced to gossip against themselves.

The monkeys throw their offspring to the tigers
as delicacies for dulled taste buds—
they have no pity for their own flesh and blood—
hunger for power has stunned their senses.

Oh, what a pity for Raja Sieha.
Why do you take refuge in the Himalayas?
You've not shown up to give us advice.
Or have we done something to offend you?

Have you noticed that the lakes have dried up?
That there's been a drought and all the fish have died?
Or is it because two shoulders now carry three stocks—
is that why you haven't shown up?

In your long absence, we wonder what's going to happen next.
Are you going to wait for the preceptor to find you and lead you back?
Or is it because you find no shade in which to stop?
Is that why you won't come back?

Why don't you have pity on our sentient beings
who have suffered untold agonies.
Nowadays we take no joy in anything,
only frustration and anguish.

And now everything goes haywire:
the crocodiles are drowning in the rivers.
Do you know that the fish are afraid of lakes,
and baby tigers are afraid of their mothers, and otters afraid of fish.

អន្ទង់ខ្លាចភក់ កុកខ្លាចបឹង   ស្វាក្រិសក្រេញីងចេះស្រជី
ឈើធំមួយដើមបដ្ឋោងបី   ទេវាប្រុសស្រីស្រឡាញ់ប្រេត ។

សំបកឈ្លោកលិចក្នុងទឹកស្រេ   អំបែងបេក បែរប្រែអណ្ដែត
នេះហើយហៅកើតកោលាហេតុ   ផ្គរលាន់ខែចេត្រភ្លៀងលិចស្រុក ។

លិចស្រេចំការ ច្បារដំណាំ   លិចប្រែកទាំងប្រាំ គ្រប៉ាងថ្ងុក
ទេបត្រីទាំងឡាយសប្បាយសុខ   ស្បើយទុក្ខរិកមុខព្រោះទឹកភ្លៀង ។

ភ្លៀងភ្លីបំផុង កណ្ដាលព្រៃ   អាលវាលដល់ដៃស្រីមានរាង
សំពត់ពេញដៃស្រីមិលោាង   ព្រោះយេីញទឹកភ្លៀងពីលើភ្នំ ។

Eels are afraid of mud, egrets afraid of ponds.
Now the little monkey knows how to talk
and there is a big tree with three ladders,
whereas men and women fall in love with ghouls.

Dried gourds sink in the paddy fields,
while broken dishes are afloat everywhere;
this is called social upheaval.
And when there is thunder in April, the rain will inundate the lands,

overflowing the paddy fields and gardens,
overflowing the five rivers, lakes, and ponds,
then the fish will become jubilant.
It alleviates their miseries; they smile because of the rain.

Some have seen a light deep in the jungles,
spreading to a lady of beautiful form.
Even though her sampot is dirty, she doesn't wash,
because torrents rush from the mountaintop.

សង្គ្រាមដណ្ដើមនាគ

ទឹកជីអង្ករសំរាប់ជីវិតសពួសត្វ
តែមិនមែនសំរាប់អ្នកឈ្លានពានឡើយ ។
ហើយទឹកជាសម្បត្តិធម្មជាតិ
ជាកម្មសិទ្ធិរបស់ព្រះ មិនមែនជារបស់អ្នកណាដែរ ។ កម្ពុជា!

ខាងជើងជាប់នឹងសាច់ញាតិ;
ខាងកើតទល់នឹងដែនយក្ស;
ខាងត្បូងសមុទ្រ;
ខាងលិចបងប្អូនបង្កើត ។

ធំទូលាយនិងរុងរឿងនាមតីតកាល;
តឲ្យវុវញត្តូចពេញដោយអ្នកលួងដំជោរ ។
សាសន៍ខ្មែរ
ប៊ិសរលត់សាប់សូន្យ ។

ម៉្យាងណាក៏ដោយទេវលោកស្ងុះប្រញ្ញាប់
ចាប់កន្ទុយនាគជាប់ ពេលអសុរឃក្តអូសក្ប្បាល
ឯព្រះនារាយណ៏កាឡ្បាជាអណ្ដើកអវតារ
ខ្នងទ្រភ្នំមន្ទះ ។

សង្គ្រាមដណ្ដើមនាគ – ទាញទៅ-ទាញមក ភ្នំមន្ទរវិល កូរវឹក
សមុទ្រទឹកដោះទៅជាទឹកអម្រឹត ។ ទំរាំបានទឹកអម្រឹត
កម្ពុជាខ្លួចខ្លាំរហេមរហាម
ដូចអណ្ដើកត្រូវភ្លើង ។

THE DISPUTE FOR THE POSSESSION OF NAGA

This land of Angkor is for all,
but not for encroachers;
and water is natural, the property
of God—not yours or mine. Cambodia!

Relatives to the North,
the giant to the East,
the sea to the South,
the full sibling to the West.

Vast and glorious in the past,
eclipsed and duped these days,
the Khmer race
seems doomed to extinction.

Nevertheless, Devalokas rush to grasp the tail of Naga,
while demons pull roughly at its head;
at the same time, Vishnu turns himself into a turtle
which holds up Muontara Mountain on its back.

The dispute for the possession of Naga
causes Muontara Mountain
to rotate and churn the Sea of Milk
until it turns to Amrita.

Until that comes to pass
Cambodia will stay bereft,
as miserable
as tortoises in a wildfire.

សច្ចាប្រណិធាន

I. មូលហេតុ

កាលនៅក្នុងខ្លួ   ស្រុកកើតទុក្ខភ័យ
សង្គ្រាមឥស្សរៈ   យៀកមិញលុកស្រុក
បារាំងអបល់ក្សណ៌   ចាប់ខ្មែរដាក់ច្រវាក់

ខ្មែរសម្លាប់ខ្មែរ ។

ខ្ញុំអស់សង្ឃឹម   មើលមេយសន្ទឹម
ព្រោះកូនអ្នកស្រែ   មិនយល់អីសោះ
តែទុក្ខឥតល្ហើ   ស្រណោះជាតិខ្មែរ

បាត់ធាតុដឹកនាំ ។

ខ្មែររស់អបយស   ពូជពង្សធ្លាប់ខ្ពស់
ផុតពីញញាំ   ឥឡូវបាត់អស់
បាត់ភាពរឹងមាំ   រស់នៅអត់ទ្រាំ

ទំរាំមរណា ។

បាត់បង់ឯករាជ្យ   រស់ក្នុងព្រួយខ្លាច
រាត្រីទិវា   បាត់សាមគ្គីធម៌
ធ្វើស្រែចំការ   ចិញ្ចឹមអាត្មា

ពុំដែលគ្រប់គ្រាន់ ។

ខ្ញុំរស់ក្នុងទុក្ខ   អាសូរភូមិស្រុក
នៅពេលផ្គរលាន់   ខ្មែរខ្ចនទទេ
ស្មារដួចសត្មាន់   ខ្ញុំប្រាក់បង់ពន្ធ

អត់ស្រែជាស្រូវ ។

OATH OF ALLEGIANCE

I. MOTIVATION

During my childhood   the country was in chaos.
It was the war of liberation   and the Viet Minh infiltrated.
The French colonialists   chained innocent Khmers
          while Khmers killed each other.

It was desperate—   I looked at the sky; it was high.
Because I was a farm child   I didn't understand anything.
Often I was miserable—   for my people,
         who had no leaders.

The Khmers lived in shame.   They were once noble,
proud, glorious,   but they had lost everything.
They'd lost human dignity.   They'd been living in fear,
         waiting for death.

They lost their independence;   they lived in anxiety and uncertainty,
day in and day out.   They lost unity.
They farmed the land;   they made a living
         but there was never enough to eat.

I lived the agony   of my people
as the earth thundered.   Khmers were half-nude—
shivering like chickens.   No money to pay taxes,
         no land to grow rice.

ខ្ញុំទ្រាំពុំបាន   កម្មញ្ញេវុញ្ញេច្រាន
នាំចិត្តត្រម្រូវ   ឲ្យងស្ងួងសច្ចា
សុំព្រះទាំផ្លូវ   ពាក្យសត្យជិតនៅ
                    ដូចតទៅនេះ ៖-

II. ពាក្យសច្ចា
បើខ្ញុំចោលម្បៀត   កុំទុករស់ទ្បេត
នាំផ្លូវផែនដី   ពន្លិចខ្ញុំចុះ
ឲ្យលិចតាមថ្ងៃ   បើនៅចត្រៃ
                    ទឹកដីគោកធ្លុក ។

ខ្ញុំមិនក្បត់ទ្បើយ   មាតុភូមិថ្ងៃអើយ
ខ្ញុំបានកើតមក   ខ្ញុំត្រូវសងគុណ
ម្ដប់ខ្ញុំបានជ្រក   បារមីដើមធ្លុក
                    ផ្ដ្រមកគោត្តម ។

បើរស់ឥតការ   រស់ឥតខ្ញុំមសារ
សូមឲ្យរបខ្ញុំ   ព្រះធរណីស្រូប
មុនពេលធាត់ធំ   កុំទុកខ្ញុំយំ
                    ស្រណោះមាតុភូមិ ។

ពេលនោះខ្ញុំ ៖
អុជធូបបិសវ៉ែស   ប៉ែរមុខចំថ្ងៃ
លើកហត្ថប្រណម្យ   សច្ចាអធិដ្ឋាន
ពិតទូលយំសុំ   ពេលថ្ងៃក្រហម
                    ព្រឹកព្រាងសូរិយា ។

សុំសេចក្ដីពិត   ម្ដេចទ្បើយជីវិត
ជនជាតិខេមរា   ជួបតែព្រាត់ប្រាស
លោកណាផ្ដាសា   ឲ្យងស្ងួងសច្ចា
                    សុំសុខជូនជាតិ ។

I could not stand it;   my commitment compelled me,
forced my will   to pronounce this oath
begging God to guide my way   with these sacred vows
                which I relate to you now:

II. PRONOUNCEMENT
"If I am a rake   let me not survive.
If I just weigh down the earth   let me drop dead.
Let me sink with the sun   if I disgrace
                this land of Kok Thlok.

I shall never betray you,   my Motherland!
I was born from your womb,   and I shall pay my debts
to the shade where I've rested,   the shade of the *thlok* tree,
                where Gautama had once sat.

But if my lot is   to lead a life of deprivation
may my body   be swallowed up by Mother Earth
before I've grown up.   Do not let me weep
                in sorrow for my Motherland."

Then, I burned three sticks of incense. Facing the Father of Life
I raised both my hands   over my head, praying to God
crying out for   the Truth
                before the revolving ember.

I cried out for the Truth: "Why are my people
always mistreated   living in a broken homeland.
Who has cursed this little nation?"   I cried out for
                Peace for my people.

—1952

បឹងក្រៀល

ព្រៃស្រលាតអន្លាយឆ្លាយផុតជើងមេឃ	ទឹកចាំងផ្លេក ផ្លេក ឃើញដើមគ្មោតរាំ
សត្វកុកក្រសាចិកត្រី គ្រុងគ្រាំ	ក្របីដល់វ័ធទ្រហឹងអឺងអាប់ ។
អាចាញ់ប្រាសបោលបែកទឹកសំពោង	អាឡ្មៀងមេហ្មូងក្បៀងញ៉ីប្រញ្ញាប់
អាស្ងាវលោតភ្លេតពាក់ញ៉ីរុញសាប់	អាឡ្មៀងវ័ធវ៉ីបំចាត់អាសៀវ ។
ត្រដេវធាបវ៉ីវចេញពីសុរិយា	កន្ទុំរុយជាច់ផ្សារចូលពួនក្រោមសេៗ
កណ្ឌូបភ័យប្រាសចូលសំងំនៅ	ក្នុងសេៗធ្លើហិ ត្រដេវហើរហួស ។
កុមារទាំងឡ្មាយទាំគូាជុំកង់	ស្វ្យៗគិឋិកតផ្ទង់លេងវែក បាយ ខុំ
ខ្លះច្រៀងសករាទ៍លើដើមឈើធំ	ខ្លះទ្រាលសំងំក្រោមមួប់ទ្រឡែ ។
លុះពេលសុរិយាជិតបាត់រស្មី	បក្សាបក្សីហើរទៅទ្រទំ
ជាហ្វូងជាផ្ងួរ តាមគូច តាមធំ	គោបាលសោាតនាំសត្វចូលក្រោលហោង ។
ពេលសន្ធិយារាត្រីដណ្ដប់វាលព្រៃ	សត្វល្អិតគឹកកែ ក្ល្មាត់ ព្រៃករំពង
តារានិករផ្លាក់ទឹករហង់	កសិករលង់លក់សុខក្នុងនិទ្រា ។

16 |

BUNG KRIEL
(THE LAKE WHERE CRANES MATE)
for Ginny Duncan

The paddy fields stretch beyond the horizon.
Where water glitters, palm trees dance.
Where egrets and herons flap after fish,
water buffalo charge each other, grunting like giants.

The losers spatter water like paddleboats going upstream.
While the old buffalo is courting his mate,
a young bull quickly mounts her—
the old bull charges and butts him away.

In the air,
the birds dive out of the sun.
Dragonflies quickly fold their wings and fall,
and grasshoppers crouch in the grass.

Boys and girls fall into small clutches—
some play reak and bikom,
some sing in the trees,
others sprawl in the shade.

When the sun streaks across the horizon,
the birds disperse and fly
in ordered flocks to their nests
and the herders lead their cattle home.

When darkness settles upon the plain
insects, geckoes, and frogs rock this kingdom.
A million stars drop everywhere,
and farmers fall asleep in peace.

ភពប្រមាញ់

គឺជាភពផ្សេកមួយ –
មានពាស់គ្រប់ប្រភេទរាប់មិនអស់
ដុកដង់ចាំយាម បំរុងចឹកខ្ញុំ
ពេលខ្ញុំធូរទិស;

វំពេចនោះ មាននារីម្នាក់ជើរទន្ធឹមខ្ញុំ
រូចនារីពីរនាក់ចេញមកទ្បៀត;
ពេលខ្ញុំលុយកាត់ភពប្រែប្រួលនេះ
ខ្ញុំគេនិយាយគ្នាពីការប្រមាញ់ ។

"អញ្ញបាញ់សត្វស្វាបឹងស្មាអញ"
នារីមាឧខ្លស់ បន្ទឹសម្លេង
រូចគេទាំងអស់គ្នាចាប់និយាយ
ពីរឿងប្រមាញ់សែនសប្បាយនៃគេ ។

យើងបានទៅដល់ភូមិមិនដែលស្គាល់មួយ
ដែលមានបក្សាបក្សីហើរជាហ្វុង
លើអ្នកប្រមាញ់ ។

ដោយផ្ដិតផ្ដង់ គេតម្រង់ទៅចំសត្វហើរ
ហើយបាញ់ធ្លាក់ខ្ទះ
នឹងស្មារបស់គេ ។

គេដោតបក្សាបក្សី
ចំបេះដួងនឹងព្រះ
ហើយទាំគ្នាសើច ។

THE HUNTING WORLD

It's a strange world—
countless snakes of all kinds
lying as sentinels, ready to strike
as I alter my course;

Suddenly a girl is walking beside me,
then two more come along;
as I wade through this fluid world,
I hear them talking about hunting:

"I shot a bird with my crossbow,"
a tall girls says,
and they all start talking
about how wonderful their hunting was.

We arrive at an unknown village
where birds fly endlessly
above the hunters;

Carefully, they aim at them
and shoot some down
with their crossbows;

They pierce
the birds' hearts and laugh.

សំណោកខ្ទោចទួញ

បងឥតដឹងខ្លួនថាត្រូវអូនបួជាទៅហើយ
ទល់បងដឹងដ៏ថាបាត់កូនដៃឆ្នេង
បងសោកយំរាប់ម៉ោង
ហើយចង់ឃើញអូនជាចុងក្រោយ ។

បងខំមកលេងនឹងអូន
សាត់តាមអាកាសថយក្រោយដូចកំសួល
ខែមេសាពេលរស្យើលស្ងប់ ហើយឃើញ
មុខផ្ទាប់ស្គាល់ជាច្រើន បប្ឫរមាត់ផ្សារជិត

ដោយមិស្យភាពឧស្យាហកម្មយោធា ។
ហើយពេលបងមកដល់មាត់ទ្វារ
ដែលផ្ទាប់តែដើរចេញចូលដោយងាយ
បែរជាភ្លាក់រន្ធត់នឹងសញ្ញាជើងក្អែកលើមេទ្វារ ។

ឱ ស្នេហ៍ អើយ!
នាងអន្ធោកអន្ធោលឲ្យបងរងសោកឥតស្រាក ។
អំណោះគតទៅ។ ភពបង ផ្សេងហើយ!
អំណោះគតទៅ។ចុងឈើជាបាទបងហ្មុតហើយ ។

ចាំស្ដាប់សំណោកបងតាមឲ្យល់ចុះ
មើលទុក្ខព្រួយបងតាមមេឃស្រទំ
ស្ដាប់ទឹកភ្នែកបងតាមរយៈទឹកភ្លៀងទៅ
ណា ស្នេហ៍សម្ឡាញ់ បង!

THE HOWLING DEAD

I didn't know you'd cremated me
until I couldn't find the little finger
of my left hand. I wailed for hours
and wanted to see you once and for all.

I came to pay you a visit,
wading backward like vapors
on a calm afternoon in April, and saw
many familiar faces with lips welded

by the military-industrial complex.
And when I arrived at your door,
which I used to pass through freely,
I was horrified by crosses on the threshold.

O, my love!
You induce in me everlasting sorrows.
Henceforth my world is different.
Henceforth I will live in the trees.

Listen to my howl through the winds,
look at my sorrows through the gray skies,
feel my tears through the rains,
O, my incomparable love!

សូមសន្តិភាពមានដល់ប្រទេសកម្ពុជា

ឱខ្មែរអើយកុំប្រែចិត្ត ឱសូមយើងគិតឲ្យវែងឆ្ងាយ
បើភូមិយើងសុខសប្បាយ សូមកុំឲ្យឃ្លាតនឹងសន្តិភាព ។

បើទឹកថ្លុកយើងនៅថ្លាថ្លង សូមយើងកុំចង់ធ្វើឲ្យល្អក់
កុំចាក់សំរាមឲ្យក្រខ្វក់ កុំចុះគ្រលុកលេងជាល្បែង ។

គេថាភ្លៀងភ្គាវាភ្គាមែន សត្វលោកគ្រប់បានដឹងប្រាកដ
មិនបាច់យើងធ្វើការពិសោធន៍ នាំឲ្យធេះខ្លោចអសោចប្រាណ ។

បើយើងកើតមកជាបញ្ញវន្ត ចូរយើងកុំភាន់ថាសាស្ត្រ
មិនចង់ឲ្យយើងសុងខ្លួនទៅ ក្នុងភ្នក់ភ្លើងភ្គាវិនាសបង់ ។

ឱបញ្ញវន្តអើយជ្រើសវិនាស កុំយករនាស់រាស់ជីលេង
ពេលស្មៅដុះខ្ជីនាវាលវែង កុំតាំងខ្លួនខែងបំផ្លាញស្មៅ ។

បានធ្វើថ្វាយសម្តេចព្រះប្រមុខរដ្ឋប្រទេសកម្ពុជា ហើយព្រះអង្គបានអនុញ្ញាត
ឲ្យបោះពុម្ពផ្សាយនៅខែមេសា ១៩៦៧ ក្នុងទស្សនាវដ្តីកម្ពុជារបស់ព្រះអង្គ ។

MAY PEACE PREVAIL IN CAMBODIA

O, Cambodians, do not change your minds.
Please think it over well—
if our home is enchanting and prosperous
why be fed up with Peace?

If the water in our pond is still transparent
please don't *try* to make it muddy;
do not litter it with trash,
and do not bathe in its waters.

It is true that fire is hot—
we all know it well;
we don't need tests to find that out—
it would consume our bodies for nothing.

Just because we are intellectuals
don't think that our enemies
don't want us to be annihilated,
don't want us to fall into the chasm of war.

O, intellectuals, don't trample the green prairies;
while the grass grows green, treasure it—
don't give yourselves medals
for laying it to ruin.

This poem was sent to the head of state of Cambodia and was published in the
magazine *Kampujea,* in April of 1967.

Part 2

❈ ❈

The Wilderness of Nightmare

APRIL 1970 – 1975

សម្រេចចិត្ត

"ខ្ញុំ មិនឲ្យរា
នឹងការទទួលខុសត្រូវឡើយ
ហើយខ្ញុំក៏មិន
សារភាពចំពោះមុខខ្លាំងដែរ ។"

ខ្ញុំខ្លាសអស់លោកអ្នកសច្ចំណាស់
ហើយខ្ញុំសូមទទួលទោស
ចំពោះជនសួតត្រង់ផង!

អវេ្រងពីដើមពង្រ
ប្រពន្ធដោះញ
គោក្រយេ៉ាក្រឡ្បាច់
ត្រពាំងពីត្បូង
អណ្ដូងពីខាងលិច
ឲ្យខ្ញុំធ្វើម្ដេច
បើ ខ្ញុំជាសត្វឆ្នា ។

DECISION

"I shall not shrink
from responsibilities
and I shall not
submit to the enemies."

I am ashamed of the Sacham,
and I feel guilty
for the innocent!

> *Your pestle is made of pong-ro wood,*
> *you married a girl with only one breast,*
> *and you own a bull whose cowlick's in the wrong place.*
> *Your pond's to the south of your house*
> *and your well's to the west.*
> *What do you think I can do about this*
> *when I'm just a cat?*

ធាតុយោរយោៃនេសង្គ្រាម

កាំភ្លើងផ្ទុះពាសពេញទគរ ៖
តាមរាលស្រែ ព្រែក ទន្លេ – ភ្នូក ធីរ-គី
នៅតាម ភ្នំ ព្រៃក្សៃព្រៃ
ភ្នូកវៀត-កុង ។

ពីព្រាំដែនម្ខាងទៅព្រាំដែនម្ខាង
វៀត កុង! វៀត កុង! វៀត កុង!
ខ្មែរ វៀត មិញ ខ្មែរ ក្រហម
ពាសពេញ ។

សម្រែកយំទ្រហោខ្លរខ្លរ ៖
សង្គ្រាម! សង្គ្រាម! សង្គ្រាម!
ភូមិនានាធះទ្រលោម
សាលារៀន វត្តអារាមទៅជាសមរភូមិអស់ ។

កសិករ – អ្នកស្ងួតត្រង់
ជាប់តែហោងស្ងួតស្ងីង; សូម្បីពាក្យមួយម៉ាត់ពីព្រះក៏គ្មាន!
កូនដៃកតកូនជ៉ា ម៉េៗ ក្បៀកតងគ្នា
ស្ងួតស្ងីងស្ងៀមស្ងាត់ សូម្បីការភ្ញ្តាក្ញ្តក៏តគមដ្ឋីមាន ។

អាគារអិដ្ឋ ផ្ទះអ្នកស្រុក ខ្ចេចអស់តែមួយយប់ ។
ហ្វូងខ្មែរក្រហមផុសចេញពីផេះ
ដូចហ្វូងរុយ
កើតចេញពីសពរលួយ ។

ប្រគតស៊ីខ្មោចមានជ័យនៅកម្ពុជាហើយ
បញ្ញាញាណ ប្រវត្តិសាស្ត្រ វប្បធមិ រលត់បាត់
អបាយមុខ នាំ
សង្គមទាំងមូលទន់ខ្សោយជើបលែងរួច ។

APRIL 1970: THE ATROCITY OF WAR

Guns boomed everywhere:
in the rice fields and rivers, Thieu-Ky;
in the mountains and jungles,
Viet Cong.

From frontier to frontier
Viet Cong! Viet Cong! Viet Cong!
Khmer Viet Minh, Khmer Rouge,
everywhere.

Bellowing with rage overhead:
War! War! War!
Villages were ablaze,
schools, pagodas, turned to battlefields.

Peasants, the innocent,
lay dead: not a word from God.
Children, mothers, side by side
lay silent, no complaint.

Buildings, houses, demolished overnight.
Gangs of Khmer Rouge rose out of the ashes
like swarms of flies
from putrid corpses.

Ghouls prevailed over Cambodia.
Providence, History, Culture perished.
Debauchery
paralyzed the entire society.

សុបិនអាក្រក់

ដេករៀន ឡ្យើងមូល
ដូចទារកក្នុងទរ
ខ្ញុំឡួងសួងសូមឱ្យគេ
កុំធ្លុងព្រាំដែនឱ្យសោះ ។

ដោយវង្វេង ខ្ញុំបែរជាឃើញខ្លួនខ្ញុំ
នៅជាយកុម្ភប្ចស្ម៉ិ
គណ្ណាលវាល ។
ហើយសន្ធឹករថក្រោះ
សូរជើងទន្ត្រាំ នៃកងទ័ព
វព្ញាយគ្រប់បន្ទាបួស្ម៉ិ ។

រំពេច សម្រែក ៖
"ចាប់វា!
ចាប់វាទាំងរស់!"
គូរវឹកឈាមខ្ញុំ
ក្បាលជង្គង់ញ័រវណ្ដំ ។

ខ្ញុំដោះអាវ
គ្របមុខខ្ញុំ
អត់ដង្ហើម
ប្ងងសួងម្ដងឡ្យេត ៖
"ឱ ព្រះជាម្ចាស់ បង្វែរចិត្តគេទៅ"

NIGHTMARE

Rolling in bed, balled up
like a baby in the womb,
I wish they would
never cross the borders.

Disoriented, I somehow find myself
at the edge of the bamboo thicket
in the open field.
And the rumble of tanks
and the tromp of soldiers' footsteps
vibrate every bamboo thorn.

Soon the shouts
"Get them!
Get them alive!"
stir my blood,
make my knees knock.

I take off my shirt,
hide my face,
embrace a bamboo stalk,
hold my breath,
wish again:
"Oh, God, change their minds!"

កាលគេចូលមកកាន់តែជិត
ខ្ញុំរុញគូចទៅ គូចទៅ
គូចល្មមចូលក្នុងបំពង់បួស្បី ចុះ ។
ហើយខ្ញុំនៅតែច្រៀងទាំងសម្លេងញ័រៗ –

"ពុទ្ធោ!"
    សន្និកស្តោ្តម្នួយទង
    អាចទ្រទឹកសន្សើមបាន
    តែទ្រអំបែងតែរមិនបានទេ!

"ធម្មោ!"
    សន្និកស្តោ្តម្នួយទងអាចទ្រសន្សើមបាន
    តែទ្រអំបែងគ្រាប់បែកអត់បានឡើយ!

As they come closer and closer
I become smaller and smaller
small enough to enter the bamboo stalk.
Yet I still chant in a trembling voice—

"Buddho!"
    A blade of grass
    may support drops of dew,
    not shards of broken glass!

"Dharmo!"
    A blade of grass may support drops of dew
    but not hunks of shrapnel!

មានតែម្ដាយទេដែលអោយទុក្ខព្រួយរហូត

ឯកោ ខ្ញុំដើរ
ទៅខ្ទមដែលយើងធ្លាប់
ជួបជុំគ្នាផឹកស្រា ស
កំសាន្តកាយ ពេលសន្តិភាពអត់សណ្ដាប់ ។

ខ្ញុំអង្គុយក្រោមដំបូលស្លឹកត្នោតដដែល
សម្លឹងទៅកោះអីអស់លោក
តែពុំយល់ដល់ម្នាក់ណាសោះ
ឮតែសំណើចក្អាកក្អាយ ។

ទីនេះ ក៏ដូច ទីណាៗឯទៀត
ទីលំនៅក្លាយជារហោដ្ឋាន
ភូមិទាំងឡាយមានតែផ្ទះសល់ជាធ្យូង
រកតែឆ្កែមួយធើថ្នាំគ្មានផង ។

មីនផ្ទុះលាន់គ្រប់ទីសទី
កាំភ្លើងធំបាញ់កក្រើកដី –
ពីព្រំដែនម្ខាងទៅព្រំដែនម្ខាង
ឡើងរញ្ជួយអស់លំអងផ្កាចំប៉ា ។

អស់មេឃជ្រក អត់ជម្រកពួន
ហើយទំនួញកុមារទាំងឡាយ
ហើយសម្រែងទ្រហោយំនៃមាតា
លេចចេញពីអគ្គីសន្ធោសន្ធៅពាសភារា-

ហើយរាងកាយអ្នក អារុសោ ពាំងគ្រាប់
ការពារយើង ហើយលោហិតអ្នក
ខ្ចាយពេញមាតុភូមិ នាំព្រលឹងខ្ញុំ
ប្ដូរផ្ដាច់លើកផ្កាម្លិះ ផ្កាឈូកទុកជាសក្ការៈ ។ –

—ខែ សីហា ១៩៧០

ONLY MOTHERS WILL EMBRACE SORROWS

I wade through solitude
to the cottage where we used to
gather to drink rice wine,
enjoying false peace.

I sit under the same palm-leaf roof,
gaze at your chairs
but see no one,
hear only your laughs.

Here, it's like everywhere else—
deserted,
villages of black roofless houses;
I don't see even one dog.

The explosions of mines,
the roaring of heavy artillery
from frontier to frontier, shake every
grain of pollen from the champa flowers.

No places to hide, no skies under which to rest;
and the moaning of children,
and the cries of mothers
out of blazing fire across the land,

And your bodies, brothers, shielding us
from the bullets, and your blood
splashing over our Mother, induce my soul
to ever worship jasmine and lotus blossoms.

—from the battlefields, during my service as
a captain in the Cambodian Army, 1970

អយ្យកោស្ដ្ងឺបំពេរ

"ចៅឆ្អើយគេងទៅ   ចៅឆ្អើយកុំយំ
ចៅឆ្អើយគេងទៅ   តានៅបំពេរ គេងទៅចៅឆ្អើយកុំខ្លាចអី
ខ្លាចត់ក្រចក   អាស្ដ អត់ភ្ក ចៅឆ្អើយកុំខ្លាចអី ។

ចៅឆ្អើយតាថាកុំទៅ   ចៅទៅត្រសង
នាំប្ដូននិងបង   ជិះទូកត្រសងឆ្លងកាត់ទន្លេ ចៅឆ្អើយឆ្លងកាត់ទន្លេ ។

កាត់វាលកាត់ព្រៃ   ចៅឆ្លងកាត់អូរ
ជ្រលងជងភ្នំ   ចៅឆ្អើយគេងក្រោមដើមព្រឹង ដើមព្រឹង ។

ចៅទៅឡ្អួតហើយ   ចៅឆ្អើយគេងក្រោមដើមដួង ដើមដួង ។
ចៅនៅមិនសុខ   ចៅឆ្អើយចៅទៅឡ្អួតណា ។

ចៅអត់ជឺងខ្ចន   ចៅគេងចៅឆ្អើយ
គេងក្រោមឈើមានស្លឹកវែងៗ   មានផ្ដែកញុំ ចុំ ។

តាហោរចៅហើយ   ចៅឆ្អើយហោរចៅឡ្ងឺងភ្នំ ចៅថាតាភូត ។
ចៅចុះហ្វត   ហ្វតទៅដល់បាតអូរ ។
ទើបចៅទ្រហោ   ចៅឆ្អើយទ្រហោហោរតា ។"

—ខែ កុម្ភៈ ១៩៧៥

36

GRANDPA SUOS'S LULLABY

"Go to sleep—sleep, grandson!
Don't cry, grandson.
Don't be afraid—the tigers have no claws
And the bull elephants have no tusks.

Grandpa told you not to run off
But all you grandchildren left—
Sailed the boat across the Mekong River,
Walked across the woods.

You grandchildren rested in strawberry shade
Then, grandchildren, you took off again—
Then you rested under the coconut leaves,
Slept under the palm fronds without a care.

O, grandson, I call you to the mountaintop—
You say that Grandpa lies,
Then you crawl down the riverbank
To the dry bed, where you cry for help."

—February, 1975

Part 3

The Kingdom Of Hell

APRIL 1975 – JANUARY 1979

បុព្វហេតុនិរាស

I. ឆ្នាំ ខាល

នៅល្ងាចថ្ងៃសុក្រមន្ទចូលឆ្នាំ ខាល
ភ្នំពេញបានអនុមោទនាសុទ្ធគ្រាប់បែកផ្ទោង
ជំនួសបុណ្យតែម្តង ។

"អាទិត! អាហេង! អាផុន! ចេញ! ចេញ!
ចេញពីផ្ទះឱ្យអស់! ទុកផ្ទះចំហទ្វារចុះ!"
ក្មួយ! ខ្មែរក្រហមធាក់ទ្វារផ្ទះគូចខ្ញុំ ។
ផាំង! អ្នកផ្ទួលផ្ទះដួលច្រដាង ជាប់នៅចានបាយ ។

ប៉ាប់ ប៉ាប់ ប៉ាប់ –
ប៉ុងៗ ប៉ុង ប៉ុងៗ
ប៉ក់ៗ ក្ទឹង! ក្ទឹង! ប៉ក់! ក្ទឹង!
សម្លេងគ្រាប់ផ្ទោងលាន់ខ្ទរចេញពីក្រោមសំយាបផ្ទះខ្ញុំ ។

ខ្ញុំលួចមើលតាមបង្អួចឃើញខ្មែរក្រហមដើររវាម ។
ខ្ញុំគ្រវែង ប៉ែអាកុល៤៥ ចោលតាមបង្អួច ។
ខ្ញុំលើកកូនខ្ញុំដាក់លើពិដាន
ហោៗប្រពន្ធខ្ញុំឱ្យឡើងតាមក្រោយ ។

យើងសម្រេចចិត្តដាប់ក្នុងអណ្តាតភ្លើងចុះ ។
យើងវុំនឹងកន្ទួលនៅលើពិដាន ហើយសំងំ ។
ប្រពន្ធខ្ញុំផ្នាក់ត្រ្រឹត : "ខ្ញុំឃើញដុំពន្លីពីអាគ្គេយ៍វិលដួចបាល់ចូលមាត់ខ្ញុំផុក ។"
"ល្ងគើ! គណ្ណាណោសិនឹងសង្គ្រោះកម្មជាមិនខាន ។" ខ្ញុំឆ្លើយ

—ទី ១៣ មេសា ១៩៧៥

PRELUDE

I. THE YEAR OF THE TIGER

On the eve of our happy new year
feasting was replaced with mortar fire
in our city of Phnom Penh.

"Tith! Heng! Phon! . . . out!
Out of your houses! Leave them open!"
Bang! The Khmer Rouge kicked in the door of my guest house.
Pank! Our tenant lay dead at his supper.

Pap—pap—pap—pap—pap
Pok—pok—pok
Pong! — — — Boeung! Pong! Pong! Boeung! Boeung!
The sounds echoed in the eaves of my house.

I peeped out the window: they had surrounded us.
I threw my .45 through the window,
hoisted my son to the roof
while my wife followed.

Deciding to be burned alive together
we wrapped ourselves in a mat on the roof
and dozed. My wife jumped awake:
"I saw a beam of light from the southeast—
it roared like a ball of lightning into my mouth."
"Good! Cambodia will be saved by Indonesia," I responded.

—APRIL 13, 1975

II. ដំណើរចេញចោលផ្ទះ

យើងដេកក្នុងរម្យរកន្លែល
ចាំងាប់ តែគ្មានអ្វីប៉ះផ្ទះយើងសោះ ។
ខ្ញុំក៏ចុះពីលើពិដាន – ម៉ោង ១០ ព្រឹកទៅហើយ ។
ខ្ញុំមើលទៅក្រោ – ផ្ទះស្ងាត់ឈឹង ។

ភ័យរន្ធត់ ខ្ញុំស្ទៀកខាខ្លី
ដោះអាវនិងស្បែកជើងចោល ។
លើកកន្ទុបអាចម៍ទូល
ដេរលបៗចេញពីផ្ទះ ។

ខ្ញុំស្មានថាបាំងខ្លួនបាត់ ។ បែរទៅខ្មែរក្រហម
សើចស្ញេញដាក់ខ្ញុំ : "ទៅត្រង់ទៅកើតទៅញ្ញោម!"
ផុតបើតិត ខ្ញុំនាំប្រពន្ធកូនខ្ញុំ
ដេរកាត់ក្រោក ប្រុងឆ្លងទៅភ្នំពេញវិញ ។

ពេលនោះ អាកន្ដុំរុយ បាញ់រះពីលើ ។
វាបាញ់ទៅខាងជើង យើងរត់ទៅខាងត្បូង
វាបាញ់ពីកើត យើងរត់ទៅខាងកើត ។
ថ្ងៃនេះយើងដេកក្នុងព្រៃ ដីជាកន្លែល មេឃជាដំបូល ។

—ថ្ងៃទី ១៤ ខែមេសា ឆ្នាំ ១៩៧៥

II. LEAVE TAKING

We stayed wrapped up like that
for eternity, but nothing happened.
I climbed down—it was 10 A.M.—
looked out, the street deserted.

Terrified, I put on worn shorts,
took off my shirt and shoes. Balancing
a bundle of soiled diapers on my head,
I stumbled out of the house.

I thought I was disguised
but the Khmer Rouge snickered at me:
"Go straight to Angkar, liberated zone, *Nhom!*"
Out of my head, I led my family into the swamps,
intending to flee to Phnom Penh.

Helicopters fired helter-skelter—
we rolled ahead of the spray,
first one way, then the other.
That was that day. We slept,
the ground our mat, the sky our roof.

—APRIL 14, 1975

III. ត្រឡប់មកផ្ទះវិញ
ផ្ទះខ្ញុំពេញណែន —
សុទ្ធតែជំទាវ
នៅតែថ្ងៃថូរ ។

បាយមិនពិសា រាខ្ទុះម្ហូប
ទឹកមិនញ៉ាំ រាខ្ទុះទឹក កក
គេដេកលើព្រៃពូកយ៉ាងខ្នែង ។

គេយកអីវ៉ាន់ខ្ញុំតាមចិត្ត
ពេលនេះហើយទើបខ្ញុំដឹងខ្លួនថា
ខ្ញុំបានចាញ់សង្គ្រាមហើយ ។

—ថ្ងៃ ទី ១៩ មេសា ១៩៧៥

III. RETURNING HOME

My house was crowded, then, with noble ladies
who couldn't eat (we had no beef or pork)
and couldn't drink (no iced tea—just well water).
They filled our bedrooms and pilfered all my books;
it was at that very moment I sensed I'd lost the war.

—APRIL 19, 1975

និរាសសាធារណរដ្ឋខ្មែរ

ពួកក្អែកបានដែចង្រែចូលដល់　　ភាពជ្រួលច្របល់ខ្វល់គ្រប់ៗប្រាណ
វាដេញពីផ្ទះផុតពីការស្ទាន　　ទ្រព្យធនប៉ុន្មានពុំបានឆក់យក ។
អ្នកឈឺនៅពេទ្យវាច្រានទម្លាក់　　អ្នកខ្វាក់បាក់ខ្វិនអស់ទីជម្រក
ស្រីសម្រាលកូនឈាមនៅខ្លោកៗ　　កូនទើបកើតមកក៏វាដេញ ។
អ្នកដើរមិនរួចពាសពេញផ្លូវ　　តម្រូវបរប៉ិលដួសច្ងូកចោលចេញ
កំទេចមិនខាតទុកមិនចំណេញ　　ពួកវាទន្ទេញ - ទន្ទេញខ្លាចភ្លេច ។

ដីបែកក្រហែង　　អាទិត្យចាំងចែង
សឹងរួញកេសា　　មនុស្សម្នារាប់លាន
ប្រជ្រៀតជាន់គ្នា　　ស្ងន់ស្ងោម្នីម្នា
ឆ្វេឆ្វាពាសទិស ។

ផ្ទូង! ផ្ទូង! ប្រែត! ប្រែត!　　សាកសពអណ្តែត
ផ្កាប់ផ្ងារស្តឹងស្តឹស　　អ្នករស់រុញគ្នា
ពពូនទយគឹស　　អស់សមជាមនុស្ស
ជាម្រឹគីម្រឹគា ។

មួយថ្ងៃម្តែម៉ែត្រ　　ដំណើរតាមហេតុ
វង្វេងគ្នីគ្នា　　ព្រាត់ប្រពន្ធបុត្រ
ព្រាត់គូសង្សារ　　រាត្រីទិវា
វង្វេងវិលវល់ ។

ស្រែកទ្ទួញទ្រហោ　　ជរាដេកថ្ងូរ
គ្មានអ្នកណាខ្វល់　　រៀងខ្លួនជ្រួលច្រាល់
ប្រឹងស្វែងឲ្យដល់　　ទីណាពុំយល់
ឲ្យផុតភ្នំពេញ ។

EXODUS

Once the Blackcrows had usurped the power
they started to evacuate people from Phnom Penh;
they threw patients through hospital windows
(women in labor and the lame), drove tanks
over them then bulldozed them under.

The sun shone bright, as if it had come close to the earth.
The ground was dried and cracked.
Millions of panicked Phnompenhards jostled each other,
desperately overflowing along prescribed routes.

Out! Out! *Phankphankphank!* My cousin's guts were hanging from his belly.
Over there! *pap—pap—*
The corpses floated face up, face down in the Bassac River—
those who refused to give up their Orient wristwatches.

> Twenty meters a day
> for the first three days
> the journey without purpose;
> lost to wife and children,
> separated from your loved ones,
> repeated night and day,
> wandering in circles.
>
> There is crying and wailing
> and the elders are groaning—
> no one bothers with them;
> everyone stampeding
> to reach a destination,
> any destination
> away from Phnom Penh.

ទិន្នញ្ញវិយោគ

បងអើយ អើយបង!

បងស្លាប់ចោលអូន	ជីវិតបងសូន្យ
ទាំងឈឺខ្លោចផ្សា	ចោលអូនឯកឯង
កណ្ដាលលំហលោកា	អូនពឹងរណោ

ពិពលនេះទៅ ។

ផ្ការូមផ្កាប់រស់	ចិត្តបងតែងស្មោះ
ស្ងួតលើអូនពៅ	ពេលនេះបងស្រៀម
ឈាមបងហូររនៅ	ជិតជាប់សាច់ពៅ

ពៅទុក្ខខ្លោចផ្សា ។

អូនខមាលាទោស	អ្វីអូនធ្វើខុស
សូមលើកទោសា	អូនកប់បងហើយ
អូនលារៀមវ៉ា	សូមអ្នកស្នេហា

ផ្ទប់សុគតិភព ។

ទាហានអាវុធក្រៅស្រែកសន្ធាប់	បាញ់រះសម្លាប់គ្មានជ័រសមុខ
ទោះស្រីមានគតិភិក៏មិនទុក	វាបាញ់សម្រុកលើស្រីល្អ។
ព្រះសង្ឃក៏វាបាញ់អត់ខ្លាចបាប	បាញ់ដួចបាញ់ចាបគ្មានស្លាប់អង្គរ
អាចមិនឲ្យបានដែជំនែងលរ	អ្នកណាអង្គរវាបាញ់ចោលមុន

បញ្ញវន្តសាស្ត្រាចារ្យនាយទាហាន	បណ្ឌាអ្នកមានទ្រព្យធនជាប់កុន
ជ្រកនៅផ្ទះខ្ញុំចាំអ្នកមានបុណ្យ	ចេញជ្ជួយដោះកុនរូចពីទោសា ។
បី-ប្រាំ-ប្រាំពីរ-ដប់ប្រាំថ្ងៃកន្លង	ស្បៀងផងក៏ស្បើយខ្លោយទាំងបញ្ញា
មើលមេយក្រឡេកដុំវិញសុំលាគ្នា	ទៅរងវេទនា ហានអវិថី ។

THE KEENING OF WIVES

O, darling, my darling!
Now you are dead.
You're shot dead . . . Buddho!
You've left me alone
in the middle of the island.
From today onward
I shall have no hope.

We used to be together,
darling—you were faithful to me,
loved me deeply.
Now you stare up at me in silence
with blood still gushing from you
sticking to my flesh.
O, my heart is broken!

May you accept my apologies
for all the wrongs I've done you.
Please do forgive me
that I have to bury you here.
Goodbye, my darling—
may your consciousness
rise to heaven!

The Blackcrow soldiers blasted everyone
without distinction: male, female, the elders,
pregnant women, children; they didn't care.
They shot even the monks, the prettiest girls.

Intellectuals, professors, politicians, generals
holed up at my house for two weeks
waiting to be rescued
but in vain—so we dispersed.

និរាសវប្បធមិ៍

ទ្រព្យមានតម្លៃបានលាក់ទុកហើយ នៅថ្ងៃពេញបូណិ៌មិ

ពិសាខចិតប្រាំចន្ទត្រង់ជាក់ ខ្ញុំជាក់អីរ៉ាន់លើរទេះអូស
ចង្ក្រានចានឆ្នាំងកាំបិតអុស អង្គរក្តូនប្រុស–បទពតបង្ខំ
ដេញចេញពីផ្ទះ ពីភ្នំពេញ ពេលចេញខ្ញុំចេញទាំងទ្រហោយំ
ខ្ញុំអូសរទេះចេញចោលទ្រនំ ងាកក្រោយខ្ញុំយំ យំស្រែកទ្រហោ
    ងាកក្រោយខ្ញុំយំ – យំស្រែកទ្រហោ ៖

"ឱគេហដ្ឋានបានឆ្នាប់មនោរម្យ កេរឱពុកខំសន្សំសាងសង់
ក្បាច់នាតព្រាសទឹកពពែធ្មិតផ្តង់ រចនាទ្រទ្រង់ទំរង់បុរាណ ។
ឱបណ្ណាល័យចេតិយកាព្យឃ្លោង អស់ពេលបានឈោងឃ្លោងឃ្លាចំណាន
ពាក្យពេចន៍កវិចារទុកទូន្មាន វត្ថុបុរាណ – ខ្ញុំលែងបានឃល់ ។
ឱភ្នំពេញឆ្មើយ-វត្ថុនិអោឋអើយ ដឹងយ៉ាងណាទ្បើយលង្ខេកសោះឱ្យល់
អង្គរបរពេលករខ្ចាយខ្ចល់ កសាងដំកល់បញ្ញាញាណខ្លួន ។"

អស់ជាមនុស្សទ្បែទហើយ ពីពេលនេះទៅគ្មានយប់ថ្ងៃទេ
ឆ្លងវាលអវីចីសែនអនិច្ចា មិនដឹងយ៉ាងណា ណាព្រះអើយ!

"ស្រណោះសម្បស្សនារីកម្ពុជា ចិន្តាមេគ្មាបុរសស្រស់សួន
ពេលនេះគ្រាច់ចរអត់ពេលដេកព្ទូន អស់អីចាំងខ្លួនគ្រាច់ផ្សងរ៉ាស្សា ។
ដើមវ៉ាងឆ្នាប់រងត្រីពងក្រាមវ៉ាង តទ្បូររៃប្រ៉ាំងវ៉ាងខ្លាចដែរណោ
អត្ថិ បន ពត-សារី បុស្បា កំទេចខេមរាទាំងវ៉ាំងទាំងភ្គោត ។"

THE FALL OF CULTURE

I hid the precious wealth,
packed the suitcases with milled rice,
packed old clothes, a small scrap-metal oven,
pots, pans, plates, spoons, an ax, a hoe,
some preserved fish in small plastic containers—
loaded it all in a cart and towed it eastward
under the full moon, May '75.

"O, home! home! the sacred ground where we lived happily,
the heritage built, bit by bit, by my father,
O, the Naga fountain with its seven heads,
preserving our tradition from days gone by.

O, Monument of Independence! O, library! O, books of poetry!
I can never chant the divinely inspired poems again!
O, quintessential words of poets!
O, artifacts I can never touch or see again!

O, Phnom Penh! O, pagoda where we worship!
O, Angkor Wat, sublime monument to the
aspirations of our ancient Khmer forefathers.
Ah, I can't see across those three wildernesses:"

I'll be nowhere,
I'll have no night,
I'll have no day anymore:
I shall be a man without identity.

"Sorrow for the Cambodian women
who were faithful to their lovers;
now they wander without sleep,
any piece of ground their home.
O, rang trees, the spawning grounds,
turned to charred stilts by the Pot-Sary conflagration.

អស់បញ្ញវន្ដអស់សាស្ត្រាចារ្យ   ចេញចោលធានីភ្នំពេញនិរាស
នាំកូនលីលាល្បីល្បើល្លួងដំធោត   ព្រោះចាញ់បោកពគទាំងប្រាជ្ញករី ។
ព្រោះប្រាជ្ញាខ្ទើទាំងរាស្ត្រទាំងស្ទេច   ចាញ់ទមិឡអប្រិយទាំងស្រីទាំងប្រុស
ខុសអើយសេនខុសនិរាសរប្បធមិ ។

Annihilate the rang trees, the sugar palms,
the Khmer Republic!"

There are no more intellectuals, no more professors—
all have departed Phnom Penh, leading children,
bereft, deceived to the last person,
from coolie to king.

និរាសកូនភ្លោះ

កត្តិកយប់ជ្រៅ ខ្យល់លាន់គគីក
ដេញ័រ អើកស្រីឈឺផ្ទៃផ្សា
រកឆ្លប់ឆ្លូបអត់ធម៌មេត្តា
ស្រវារកត្រៃ ត្រៃនៅទីឆ្ងាយ ។
ឆ្លបមួយលួកខ្លះឆ្លបមួយរញ្ជ្រាន
ខ្លះយកកូនបានខ្លួបកូនចោលម្ចាយ
កូនអើយអភ័ព្ធខុសពីទំនាយ
កើតក្នុងផ្ទៃម្ចាយពុំបាននៅរស់ ។
កូនភ្លោះសែនស្រស់សុទ្ធសីងនារី
យប់ពេញបុណ្ណិមិ កូនទទួលគ្រោះ
ឱសែនគត់សូតបាត់ស្មារតីអស់
ទោះមានរបស់ក៏នឹកមិនឃើញ ។

"តា នេះកូន! យកទៅកប់ទៅ!"
ឆ្លបហុចកញ្ចប់សពកូនឲ្យខ្ញុំ ។
ប្រមាត់ក្រឡាប់ចាប់ចុកឧរា
ដល់ច្រាំងទន្លេ ខ្ញុំមើលព្រះខែ –

"កូនអើយ អើយកូន ជីវិតកូនសូន្យ
មុនឃើញសូរិយា ទុក្ខឱសែនធ្ងន់
ស្រណោះកូនភ្លា បុត្រីទ្វេហារ
ចាកលោកចោលឆី ។

ទីនេះហើយកូន ជាទីស្ងាត់សូន្យ
ជាទីកូននៅ ឱលាកូនចុះ
ឱលាកូនទៅ ឱគតទិជេrv
ទេណាកូនណា ។

ឱសុំពឹង លើមាសប្រលឹង
រាត្រីទិវា ជួយនាំផ្លូវឱ
ជួយថែមាតា ជួយដឹកដែប៉ា
ឆ្លងផុតវាលបី ។

ជួយនាំផ្លូវប៉ា ជួបរគនត្រៃ ។"

THE LOSS OF MY TWINS

Deep one night in October, '76
when the moon had fully waxed,
it was cold to the bone;
that's when my wife's labor pains began.

I searched for a bed, but that was wishful thinking;
I felt so helpless. Two midwives materialized—
one squatted above her abdomen and pushed,
the other reached up into my wife's womb and ripped the babies out.

What a lowing my wife put up
when she gave birth to the first twin.
"Very pretty, just as I'd wished, but those fiends
choked them and wrapped them in black plastic.

Two pretty girls . . .
Buddho! I couldn't do a thing to save them!"
murmured my mother.
"Here, Ta!" the midwives handed me the bundles.

Cringing as if I'd entered Hell,
I took the babies in my arms
and carried them to the banks of the Mekong River.
Staring at the moon, I howled:

"O, babies, you never had the chance to ripen into life—
only your souls look down at me now.
Dad hasn't seen you alive at all, girls . . .
forgive me, daughters; I have to leave you here.

Even though I'll bury your bodies here,
may your souls guide me and watch over your mother.
Lead us across this wilderness
and light our way to the Triple Gem."

ម្នាស់បងផ្លូវក្នុង និង ទោសសំឡេះ

ហួងអ្នកទោសជេរវប៉ាត់រប៉ាយ
ត្រូឡប់ទៅការដ្ឋានលើកទំនប់
ព្រែក តា កែវ វិញ ក្រោយការបង្ក្រ
ឆោយបោះឆ្នោតតំណាងរាស្ត្រ ខែ មេសា' ៧៦ ។

ឱកូនភ្លោះខ្ញុំអើយ!
ប្រសិនបើព្រះទុក្កូនឡ្យនៅរស់
ឱមានសំណាងណាស់មើលទៅ –
ទំនាយម្នាស់បងសុវណ្ណមាលា បុត្រាតាត្រសក់ផ្ដើម ។

ខ្ញុំកាប់ជីជាក់បង្គ្
វែកតគេៈគតៈ
ឡ្យឹងលើទំនប់
កាន់តែខ្លស់ទៅ ខ្លស់ទៅ ។

"អញ្ជាកវី សមាជិកសភា
ជាលេខាធិការឯកសារសម្ងាត់នៃសង្គមសាធារណរដ្ឋ
មានគោលនយោបាយច្បាស់
ពីសិទ្ធិសេរីភាព លទ្ធិប្រជាធិបតេយ្យ –

សុខុមាលភាពប្រជាជនកើតចេញ
ពីកម្មសិទ្ធិឯកជន មិនមែនពីការងារបង្ខំឡ្យើយ!"
អារម្មណ៍ទាំងនេះធ្វើឡ្យខ្ញុំស្រងូតស្រងាត់
នាំឡ្យមេក្រុមគោះប្រដ្ជុំជីវភាពភ្លាម ។

អាហាទេយ្យុំលើកសរសើរ អង្គការ ទុកជាព្រះអាទិទេព
ហើយលើកឡ្យឹងថាហេតុអីបានជាសមមិត្តខ្លះមិនពេញចិត្តឡ្យក
"មិនឃើញទេឬ អង្គការ កំទេចចក្រពត្ត ឥឡូវឯងរាជ្យម្នាស់ការ ។"
ខ្ញុំឆ្លើយ "ទោះក្របីក៏វានឹកកូនវាដែរ ។"

MY INVISIBLE SISTERS
AND DEATH BY EXECUTION

The horde of prisoners
returns to the dam-building site
out near Prek Ta Kao
after *élection forcée,* April, '76.

My twins! O my twins!
If you'd been allowed to live
I would have met great fortune—that's what
Sovanna Mealea, son of the Ta Trasak Phem told me.

I chop the ground, put it in two shallow baskets
balanced on a pole over my left shoulder,
and carry it to the dam,
which is getting high now.

"I'm a poet, member of the National Assembly,
member of the Steering Committee of the Social Republican Party,
which has political guidelines that
freedom, democracy, and the welfare of Cambodian society

must be born from private enterprises,
not from forced labor—"
these factors render my physiognomy suspicious.
Then one night a devil calls for a session of autocriticism.

The devil praises Angkar as higher than God,
and asks why some of us are not satisfied
when it is clear that Angkar has been serving sangkum.
"Even water buffalo take care of their own offspring!

ខ្ញុំអាចឆ្លើយតែប៉ុណ្ណោះ
ហើយខ្ញុំដាក់ខ្លួនដាក់កាយ
ជូន អង្គការ ដ៏ាក់ទិសតែប្រែ
ឲ្យខ្ញុំបានបំផេ អង្គការ កាន់តែប្រសើររឿង ។

ក្រោយសុបបរឡូច
អង្គការ ឲ្យច្បាប់ខ្ញុំទៅជួបគ្រួសារ
រទេះគោមួយនៅរង់ចាំខ្ញុំ
អរណាស់ ខ្ញុំហក់ឡើងជិះរទេះគោភ្លាម ។

58 |

តាមផ្លូវទៅជំរំ
អ្នកបររទេះហុចទឹកភ្លោតផ្លូវឲ្យខ្ញុំមួយត្រឡោក
យើងចាប់ផ្ដើមនិយាយពី សម្ដេច
"ស្ដេច បានប្រាប់យើងហើយថាបើក្ងូនចោងចង់ចូល កុម្មុយនិស្ត ស្ដេចចូលមុន ។"

ពេលទៅដល់ជួបគ្រួសារ
មានរទេះគោមួយទៀតរង់ចាំ –
"ប្រញាប់ឡើង តា យកអីវ៉ាន់លឿៗ ។"
រហ័សដូចខ្យល់ គោបោលក្នុង កាត់រាត្រី ។

ទាំងអ្នកមូលដ្ឋានទាំងអ្នកថ្មីឈរមហង់មើលយើង
ពេលយើងចេញដំណើរតែដើងច្បាស់ថាទៅភូមិថ្មី
គោបោលយ៉ាងលឿនទៅមុខ
កាត់ស្បែងដ៏តក្នុងព្រៃស្ងសាន ។

ងងឹតសួរ្យរកចំណាំអីពុំបាន
"ដល់ហើយតា!
យកអីវ៉ាន់ឡើងលើផ្ទះនោះទៅ
ខ្ញុំសង់ផ្ទាល់ដៃខ្ញុំ មុន តា មកដល់ ។"

That's all I have to say about it.
Now I shall offer my body and soul
before Angkar for judgment
so that I can be the best of servants.

After evening gruel,
Angkar orders me to join my family.
An oxcart is ready.
I jump on it, light-headed.

On the way to my shelter
the driver offers me a coconut shell of sour palm juice.
We start to chatter about Samdech Euv.
"Samdech warned us about this in the late '60s!" I tell him.

When I reach my family
another oxcart is waiting—
Hurry, Ta! Load your stuff!
As in a whirlwind, we're taken somewhere else.

Base people, new people, stand up startled
as we pass, knowing where we're headed.
The oxen gallop forward
through the dark across the jungle.

It's so dark I can't get any bearings.
"Here you are, Ta—
bring your things to that house—
I built it myself before you arrived."

អត់ស្ម៉ី អត់អរគុណ – ខ្ញុំយកកម្មសិទ្ធិសមរម្យ
ដាក់លើមន្ទីរថ្ម ៥ម x ៦ម មានផ្ទះបាយខាងក្រោយបែបបុរី
ខ្ញុំឃើញចំការពោតច្បាស់ក្រោមពន្លឺតារា
លាតសន្ធឹងខាងក្រោយខ្នម – ទន្ទេមេតដ្ឋខាងមុខ ។

"សុបិនខ្ញុំបានសម្រេចមែន : ទឹក អុស ត្រី ។"
ខ្ញុំនិយាយប្រាប់គ្រួសារ ខ្ញុំ ។
"ម៉ែ! ង៉ៃឆ្នាំងទៅ ខ្ញុំទៅវែកទឹក ។"
យើងបានទុកឆ្នាំងអាលុយមីញ៉ម ២០៣ និង ប៉ោត មួយ ។

យើងកំសាន្តបានពីអាទិត្យ
ពេលព្រឹក ខ្ញុំទៅរកត្រី
ពេលទំនេរយើងអង្គុយត្របាមក្បាលជដ្ឋង់
សំឡឹងម្ចាស់បងប្រទាល ។

ខ្ញុំលាក់ព្រះពុទ្ធរូបបាហ្គោឌីតលើមេជំបូល
ហើយទុកម្ចាស់បងប្រទាលក្នុងមុងពេលថ្ងៃ
យប់កាលណាយកលោកជាក់ហាលសន្ទើម
"ខ្ញុំឃើញអ្នកតាមអង្គុយលើជំបូក

បញ្ឈរជដ្ឋង់ម្ចាង
ក្ត ស្ដោកប៉ុនជបស្រា
ហើយនិយាយថា : "ទៅណាក៏ដោយ
ចាៗថ្ងាយអំពីលយើងមួយក្បូរ ចាៗសុខសប្បាយហើយ ។"

ប្រពន្ធនិយាយប្រាប់ខ្ញុំកណ្ដាលយប់
"ទៅបេះថ្ងាយទៅ! ខ្ញុំឆ្លើយ
ព្រឹកឡើងខ្ញុំទៅបេះផ្កែអំពីលមួយក្បូរ
យកទៅដាក់លើជំបូក សុំស្រណុកសុខសប្បាយ ។

No talk, no thanks, I bring my belongings
to the new shelter, five meters by six meters, with open kitchen.
By starlight I can see a vast cornfield
spread behind it, the Mekong River in front.

"My wish come true: water, firewood, fish,"
I tell my family.
"Mom, you cook rice, I'll go fetch water."
We'd kept a twenty-liter bucket and a twenty-liter cooking pot.

We enjoy our summer resort for two weeks.
In the mornings I go to find fish.
Otherwise, we just sit around bewildered
at how our invisible sisters have cared for us.

I hide my Buddha made of pagodite on the roof
and my invisible sister in the mosquito net by day
and out in the dew at night.
"I saw a naked man sitting on a termite mound,

one of his legs folded under him, the other bent at the knee,
and his penis big as a liter bottle,
and he said, 'Wherever you go, if you give us a green sour
tamarind fruit, grandchild's family will be safe.'"

My wife tells me this when we wake up the second morning
of our stay. "So we'll do it!" I tell her.
I climb into the tamarind, pick one fruit, and
put it on a nearby termite mound, praying for security.

អង្គការ មិនដឹងយើងនៅទីនេះនៅឡើយទេ
ខ្ញុំដើរឥកនេះ ឥកនោះ ចាប់ត្រីប្រឡាក់ ពេលថ្ងៃ
យប់កាលណាល្ងួនចូលមុងដូចពស់
យល់សប្តិទៅភ្នំពេញ – ចូលរួមមហាសន្និបាតសភា ។

ខ្ញុំស្គាល់សមាជិកតិចណាស់
ភាគច្រើន សមាជិកថ្មីៗ – ប្រធានសភា
ខ្លៅគ្រាក់ មាឍខ្លស់ដំបង –
មនុស្សម្តែនាក់ច្រានមិនរផ្តើផង ។

សមាជិកម្នាក់ៗឡើងលើវេទិកាតាមលេខរៀង
វាហារពីស្តីខ្ញុំស្តាប់មិនបាន
ទិបញ្ចប់ប្រធានវាសដៃ និយាយភ្ញែងៗ ៖
"អាណាបាចអំណាចដោយហឹង្សា វាធ្លាក់វិញក៏គ្រមាំងគ្រមោកដែរ ។"

ខ្ញុំ ភ្ញាក់ឡើង នៅក្នុងមុង
ឯជំវិ ប៖ លាវ សោ៖
ខ្ញុំ ហ៊ក់វិឯ ទៅ យកម្នាស់បងប្រទាល
មកដាក់ទុកឯអាសនៈវិញ ។

ឥឡូវ អង្គការ ដឹកប្រជាជនថ្មីចិន-ខ្មែរ មកឡៀត
"ពិណាឯ្យ តា ឯឯទៅ?" អង្គការសួរខ្ញុំ
"សមមិត្ត អង្គការ ព្រែកតាអាំ ដឹកខ្ញុំមកកន្លះខែហើយ"
ខ្ញុំឆ្លើយទាំងឈ្លោកមុខ ។

អង្គការ ប៖ លាវ ស្រឯំឈ្លោ៖គ្រសារខ្ញុំ
យើឯទទួលបានរបបស្រួមម្ងួយឯទៀឯរាល់ខែ ។
អង្គការបែចកជា ដប់នាក់ មួយក្រុម
ដំបូឯគេដាក់ទិសឱ្យខ្ញុំកាប់ ស្លឹកទ្រាំឯ ។

The Angkar of the village doesn't know we're here.
I wander during the day, finding fish that we'll preserve.
At night, we sneak among the mosquitoes like snakes.
I'm invited to Phnom Penh for an extraordinary Congress:

I recognize some of my colleagues, but the majority
of the congress is all strange—the Chairman is
two meters tall, dark skin, strongly built;
Twenty men of my size cannot budge him.

Each member of the congress takes his turn
at the podium to speak about what I don't hear.
Finally, the Chairman raves: "Whoever ascends
to power by violence, he will be overthrown by violence!"

When I open my eyes, I'm in the mosquito net
at Boh Leav concentration camp.
I go outside to recover my invisible sister,
taking her inside to her hidden sanctuary.

New people are brought to my concentration camp.
"Who let you stay here, Ta?" Angkar asked me.
"Comrade Angkar of Prek Ta Am put us here two weeks ago,"
I say, without looking at their faces.

The Angkar of Boh Leav lists the names of my family.
We get thirty kilograms of unhusked rice a month.
Angkar divides us into groups of ten.
They put me to work again, gathering palm fronds.

ទុត-តារា គ្រូអង់គ្លេសវិទ្យាល័យ ស៊ុ សុវត្តិ
ជាដៃគូខ្ញុំគ្រោយស្ម៉ា ភូរវស្រ ពេលថ្ងៃ
យប់ៗ យើងជាក់រហ៉ាត់ទាញទឹកជាក់វ្រែ
យើងច្រៀងជាភាសាអង់គ្លេស – បំភ្លេចទុក្ខ ។

"តា សាមៀន តាសាមៀន! ផ្ទះហ្ដីងឬផ្ទះ តា សាមៀន?"
"ទេ ផ្ទះ តា សារ័ណ្ណ ទេ តើ!"
គ្រួសារខ្ញុំធ្លៀយគប អង្ការ ។
"រៀបអ៊ីវ៉ាន់ ទៅមុខទ្យេត!"

64 ព្រះចន្ទចាំងគ្រចៈលើវាលព្រៃល្អប់
អគ្រាត្រទៅហើយ ពេលសម្រែកបំបែកភាពជ្រងំ
"តា សារ័ណ្ណ! តាសារ័ណ្ណ! អ៊ី តា សា រ័ណ្ណ!
ប្រញាប់ទៅ រៀបអ៊ីវ៉ាន់ ទៅមុខទ្យេត!"

កម្មសិទ្ធិសមរម្យខ្ញុំគ្រៀមជានិច្ច
យើងផុកអ៊ីវ៉ាន់លើរទេះ
អ្នកបររទេះដឹកយើងទៅជំរំថ្មីទ្យេត –
ទុកផលាទាំងឡ្បាយឲ្យ អង្ការ ។

My partner is Nuth Dara, English teacher, Sisowath High.
We clear swamps, plow fields, transplant rice
during the day, pedal water mills at night.
We both enjoy humming in English.

"Samoeurn! Samoeurn! Does Samoeurn live in this house?"
No, Ta Gold lives here. No Samoeurn here."
My wife dreams that Angkar shouts:
"Pack your stuff! Angkar orders this family forward."

The moon shines brightly over the swamps.
It's midnight when the screams break the silence—
"Ta Gold! Ta Gold! Heh, Ta Gold!
Get up and pack your stuff, Ta."

By now our stuff is perpetually ready.
We load it onto the same oxcart, it seems.
The driver takes off to another camp,
leaving the fruits of our labor for Angkar.

ពស់វែកក្របី និងអ្នកទោសសង្គ្រាម

ផែនការ ផែនការ កាប់គាស់ កាប់ឆ្ការ
ធ្វើស្រែ ចំការ ពុំមានទំនេរ
នាពេលថ្ងៃត្រង់ ឆ្លាយពីពួកគេ
ខ្ញុំឆ្ការព្រៃស្ងាត់ ក្នុងបឹង ថែស្រូវ ។

ពស់វែកក្របី សម្ដែងបុច្ឆា
បើកវែកកម្មា ស្ងានខ្ញុំសត្រូវ
"ស្ងាត មែន! ដូចកុន ឆណ្ណាពិតគន្លូវ" ខ្ញុំលាន់មាត់
ជង្គង់ ខ្ញុំកូរ ញ័រញ្ញាក់ ញ្ញាក់ញ័រ ។

"ឱនាគ! ឈាមនាគ សាច់នាគ នាគពិត
សាច់ឈាម សិន្ធុ គោត្តម ព្រះពុទ្ធ
អញ ពិត អ្នកទោសសង្គ្រាម ទេតើ
អញ សោកពុំមែន អាហារនាគឡើយ ។

នាគនាម នាគមាន សេរី
បើ អង្កុលអញពិត សាច់ឈាម នាគថ្ងៃ
នាគឆើយ មេត្តា ពិតទួល ទេព្ដាព្រឹក្សព្រៃ
ដឹកនាំអញផ្លូវ: ពុទ្ធ ធម្ម សង្ឃ ឆងណា!"

សម្លក់ សម្ដឹងចំខ្ញុំ ដោយចិត្តមេត្រី
នាគ ឱនសិរសី ចូលព្រៃ តាមធម្មទេសនា
ផ្គោះទក្សិណាទិស ខ្ញុំផុតភ័យា
បន្តការងារ ទ្រាំរស់ ត ទៅៗ ។

—ការដ្ឋានការងារបង្ខំ បុះលាវ ស្រុក ក្រចេះ វិច្ឆិកា ១៩៧៦

WATER BUFFALO COBRA
AND THE PRISONER OF WAR

for Gregory Ann Smith

Work, work—hacking at trees, uprooting them, clearing bushes,
transplanting rice, no time to rest.
At noon, alone, as I cleared the canebrake,
a beautiful black cobra

opened his hood before me, displaying his power.
He thought I was his foe.
"He's beautiful, just like in the Indian movies!"
I exclaimed to myself while my knees knocked.

"O, cobra! Your flesh and blood are truly
Buddha's flesh and blood.
I am just a prisoner-of-war,
but I am not your food.

You, cobra, are free,
and if my flesh is truly your blood,
plead my case with the spirits of this swamp
to lead me to Buddham, Dhammam, and Sangham."

The cobra stared at me with loving kindness
then lowered his head.
He slithered into the swamp to the south,
and I went back to my work of surviving.

—Boh Leav Concentration Camp, Kratie, November, 1976

ម្រេញគង្វាលលេងលាក់កូន និង ក្របី

I.

ពីយប់ម៉ោងប្រាំ ដល់ ថ្ងៃម៉ោងដប់
ខ្ញុំឈប់សំរាកក្របីទាំងគូ
ឲ្យវាស៊ីស្មៅៗ ខ្ញុំទៅដងអូរ
ដងទឹកយក មក អោយកូនប្រពន្ធ ។

ធ្វើការនេះនោះ ពុំបានគិតដល់
ចិត្តតែងអំពល់ខ្វល់គ្មានស្រាកស្រាន្ត
យប់ថ្ងៃមើលមេឃ ដឹងពេលណាបាន
ផូវក្តីសុខសាន្ត បានរួចទោសា ។

រសៀលម៉ោងបី រក្របីទីម
ក្នុងចិត្តសង្ឃឹម បង្អើយកិច្ចការ
បាចជីស្រែផ្សោលជាងប្រាំហិតា
ព្រែកងសល់ពេលា បានលេងនឹងកូន ។

រកមើល មីខោល បាត់ស្រមោលឈឹង
មិនដឹងវាស៊ីត្រង់កំពោតណា
"អាម៉ាប់ ឯងឃើញ មីខោល ដែរទេ?"
ខ្ញុំស្រែកសួរវាទាំងភ័យរន្ធត់ ។

ខ្ញុំលោតឡើងផង៖ លើខ្នង អាម៉ាប់
សន្ទាប់ប្រញាប់ បំបោលផ្នោតៗ
អាម៉ាប់ នាំខ្ញុំរកគ្រប់កំពោត
ពុំឃើញ ខ្ញុំលោតចុះទៅរកកូន ។

THE ELVES CONCEAL MY BUFFALO AND MY SON

for Ken McCullough

I.
I work from 3:00 A.M. to 10:00 A.M.
before I rest my buffalo
so that they might browse while I go
fetch water for my wife and son.

I keep busy at this and that,
not thinking about my buffalo—
I'm obsessed, night and day, looking
for peace to quell these agonies.

At 3:00 P.M., I look for my
buffalo to hitch them up and
fertilize five hectares of paddy fields,
leaving time to play with my son.

But I can't find Shorthorns—I search
every thicket, but she's nowhere.
I ask Fat Boy, "Where is Shorthorns?"
with a catch of fear in my voice.

Then I vault onto his back and
slap him to a gallop with my feet.
We search high and low—not a trace.
Then I hop down to find my son.

ក្របិ ក៏បាត់ កូនសោត ក៏បាត់
ពេលនេះមុខព្រាត់ ជីវិតខ្ញុំសូន្យ
ខ្ញុំប្រាសរត់វឹង ចូលព្រៃរកកូន
"អើយ កូន! អើយ កូន! កូនទៅទិណា?"

ខ្ញុំរត់ទៅឧត្តរ ស្រែកហៅរកកូន
កាត់ព្រៃស្ងាត់សូន្យ ស្រែកហៅបុត្រា
ខ្ញុំរត់កាត់ទឹក កាត់ព្រៃព្រឹក្សា
យំស្រែកទ្រហោ រំពងព្រឹក្សព្រៃ ។

"កូនប្រុសសំឡ្យាញ់ – បាត់ទៅទិណា –
សូមអស់ទេព្តារក្សាដែនដី
ជួយរកកូនខ្ញុំ ទាន់ពេលនៅថ្ងៃ
អយ្យកោ កោសិយ បិតានាគធង

ម្ចាស់បងក្រមុំ ពិជោរមានបុទ្ធិ
បូរីឥន្ទនិម្មិត អ្នកតាជ្រលង
ជងអូរព្រៃភ្នំ អ្នកតាស្រុកភ្នង
ព្រមអស់ម្ចាស់បង ក្រពុំឈ្មក ក្រពុំធេះ –

សូមជួយនាំផ្សវ អោយចៅជួបបុត្រ
អោយចៅរួចផុតទោសកាប់សំឡេះ
អយ្យកោសូស្ត៍ហោង ជួយដោះខ្ញុំម្ចាស់
ឲ្យចស្រម្យះ ទោសងាប់តាយហោង – !"

ត្រឡប់ដល់ខ្មម កូនកំពុងលេង
"មីខោលទៅណា ព្រលឹង យើញទេ?"
"អត់ដឹងទេ៎ ខ្ញុំលេងនឹងគេ
តាំងពីថ្ងៃព្រជ ក្រង់តែទីនេះ!"

The she-buffalo has vanished.
So has my son. Now my life *is*
over. I shout through the forest:
"Oeuy, son! *Oeuy,* son! Where have you gone?"

To the north, I cry for my son;
I cry all through the mute jungle.
Wading through dismal swamps, I cry
at the top of my lungs for him:

"O, son whom I love, where are you?
O, devas, spirits of the trees,
find my son before the sun sets.
Grandpa Kosei! Father Naga!

Princess Kramum! Pido Mean Roeuddhi!
Borei Indranimitta! Phnong
spirits of this dell! Krabum Chhouk
and Krabum Chheh, my elder spirits,

Please guide me to my son, please save
me from my own execution!
O, Grandpa Suos, I implore you,
lead me from a violent death!"

I quit and return to my shack.
My son is playing by the door.
Has Proloeung seen Shorthorns?
"I've been here with *them* the whole time."

II.

សូរិយាចូលព្រៃ រាត្រីចេញយាម
អ្នកចាស់មូលដ្ឋានស្រែកប្រាប់គ្នាថា៖
"ក្របីតាហ្គោល ស៊ីស្រូវដប់ជារ!"
នេះពិតពួកវា ចង់វៃខ្ញុំចោល ។

III.

ម៉ោងប្រាំបួនព្រឹក មេកងចាត់ការ
ឲ្យរៀបអាហារ ឲ្យខ្ញុំយ៉ាងឆ្ងាញ់
បាយស្រួយ សាច់នោរ ត្រីផ្អក់ ត្រីក្រាញ់
ឆ្ងាញ់ឆើយសេនឆ្ងាញ់ បិឆ្នាំ ទើបបានស៊ីម្ងង ។

ពេជយាតស៊ីវែរ ខ្មែស្ងាយពាក់ឆ្បៀង
មាត់ស៊ី ភ្នែកដេវៀង មើលខ្ញុំ ម្ងង១
កំពុងតែស៊ី មិខោាល ជើបធ្មោល
ពេជយាត មេកង ចុងភៅ សើចគីល ។

"តាហ្គោល សំណាងម៉េន មេកងវាចា
កុំអីច្បាស់តា ផ្ទុបស្រុក ស ឆ្លិង ។"
ខ្ញុំនៅពុំយល់ ខ្ញុំធ្វើ ពុំដឹង
ខ្ញុំឱំតែប្រឹង ស៊ីបាយទល់ផ្អែត ។

—ស្រែព្រៃង យ៉ុំចឹង ស្រុកស្មួល ក្រចេះ មិថុនា ១៩៧៧

II.
The sun sinks; the night takes over.
Old People shout to each other:
"Grandpa's beast ate an acre of shoots!"
—just the evidence they need.

III.
At nine the next morning, the chief
tells the field kitchen boss to cook
steamed rice with fried carp for me—Ahh!
—my first decent meal in three years.

The executioner, cord coiled
round his shoulder, stares while we eat
in silence. Then Shorthorns appears!
Everyone falls over laughing!

"Grandpa Gold is lucky! He almost
traveled to the white bones village!"
I feign not knowing what they mean
and keep stuffing myself with rice.

—Sre Pring, Choeung, Snuol, Kratie, June, 1977

សុបិននៅផ្សោល យុំចឹង ស្ងួល ក្រចេះ

ព្រលឹមម៉្មោងបីក្រោកដំរង់ផ្ទុរ
មេកងចេញស្ងួរ រាប់ក្បាលមុនចេញ
ទៅស្រែច្រកកាត់ស្ងួរទុំពាសពេញ
គិតតែចំណេញ ន្ហុះ បក្សកុម្មុយនិស្ត ។

ម៉្មោងប្អូនងឹតចេញចាប់ធ្វើការ
រជួរធ្ងា ច្រតស្ងួរទាន់ព្រឹក
ផ្គាមញ់រវណ្ដំ ដែលញ់រអឹក
ច្រតហើយត្រូវដឹក គរទុកបោកយប់ ។

បបរឆ្អួចហើយ ប្រជុំជីវភាព
ដាក់ខ្ទនសារភាព ផ្ទនដល់អង្គការ
ចាខ្ញុំប្រឹងណាស់ បើខុសគ្រង់ណា
សម្បហាភាពមេគ្នាផ្ទួយស្ដីផ្ទួយតែ ។

ក្រោយជីវភាព យើងចាប់បោកស្ងួរ
មេកងតម្រូវបោកស្ងួរឲ្យហើយ
អផ្ទាគន្លងផុត ស្ងួរនៅទេឡើយ
ដល់បោកស្ងួរហើយ ខ្ញុំហារទន់ខ្លួន ។

ប្រាសខ្ទនដល់ជី លក់អត់ដឹងប្រាណ
វិញ្ញាណ៍ចេញជីរឆ្ពោះទិសបូព៌ា
ដល់ខ្ទមគូចម្ងួយ យើញតែតាតា
ពិតជាទេព្យរក្សាព្រឹក្សព្រៃ ។

តាដេញចាប៉ុ ដេញសែនស្រណោះ
តាច្រេវៀងពីរោះ គូរឲ្យចាប់ចិត្ត
ឈរស្ងាប់ឃ្មួរៗ ខ្ញុំទឹកអាណិត
ជាតិខ្ញុំជាជាតិ មិនដែលស្គាល់សុខ ។

DREAM AT PHTDOWL
CONCENTRATION CAMP

3:00 A.M.—it's time to get up
and stand in rows, for the chief
of the camp to count our heads;
to him, we're just a source of income.

4:00 A.M.—still dark, the work starts;
in the cold, we harvest the rice paddy.
Our teeth chatter, our hands shiver.
After harvest, we lug the bundles for threshing.

At night, after gruel, we have a "life" meeting
to confess and let Angkar correct us: "I've
worked hard . . . if I have more faults, may samohapheab
chastize me and set me on the right path!"

After the meeting we thresh the rice.
The chief orders us to finish in a night;
midnight slips by, yet the bundles seem to multiply.
After threshing, I'm exhausted.

Once my back is on the ground, I pass out.
My soul walks east to a small shack
low to the ground where two middle-aged men
sit face-to-face. They must be gods of the forest.

One man plays a long-stringed guitar,
the other sings melodiously.
As I stand there listening, I feel despair
that my people have never met peace.

ពេលនោះខ្ញុំចូលច្រៀងដែរ-៖ –

"ឆើយ – មើលចុះ – ទេព្តារក្សាទឹកដី
ជាតិខ្ញុំប្រុសស្រី វេទនាក្រេណា –
ទាំងយប់ទាំងថ្ងៃ ខំប្រឹងធ្វើការ
ហុតទឹកបបរ នៅតែមានទោស ។

សូមព្រះជាម្ចាស់ បើកទិព្ទចក្ខុ
ទតចុះកម្ពុជា – សូមព្រះជួយច្រោស
សត្រូវទន្ធធ្ងន់ ៖ ក្នុងចាស់ស្រីប្រុស
ព្រះឆើយជួយច្រោសរូបឆុតទុក្ខភ័យ ។"

ខ្ញុំច្រៀង – ស្រុកច្រៀង – ផ្ទុកខ្មែរ បិសាច
ញាក់ញ័រ ញ្រ័ញ្រាក់កន្ត្រាក់ជើងជើរ
ច្រងេង ច្រងាង ក្រទិក្រទា
ឈរជើងក្រោយពីរ លោតចេញពីចាស ។

ខ្ញុំច្រៀង-ប្លុងស្ងួងអស់ព្រះមានបុឡ្ឌិ
ជួយស្រង់ជីវិត ផុតក្តីវិនាស ;
បាលក្នុងពីក្បូង ចេញសត្រូវមាស
បាលបុស ចំ ពោះ ផ្ទុកខ្មែរបិសាច ។

ខ្ញុំច្រៀង ស្រុកច្រៀងរផ្ទើប្រឹក្សប្រៃ្រ
ផ្ទុកខ្មែរ + រមាស ផល់គ្នា – សាហារអស្ចារ្យ ;
រមាសបុសផ្ទុក ត្រវាត់ទៅលើ – ធ្លាក់វិញជាច់ផ្សារ ;
ខ្ញុំឆ្នាក់កាលណា សូរិយាក្រង់ជាក់ ។

—តុលា ១៩៧៧

Then I join the singing:

"Oeuy—look down on us, oh gods of the land!
My people, men and women, suffer beyond words.
They work hard day and night,
they slurp gruel, yet they *still* bear faults.

Open your magic eyes, God-Father!
Look at Cambodia! Liberate my people!
They are in Hell: children, elders, men, women.
Oh, God, free us from agony and fear!"

I sing and sing in a loud voice, until
a roast pig with its front gaping open
stands up trembling, swaggers around on its
hind legs and jumps from the tray.

I sing to invoke the almighty gods to
save my people from extinction. And just then
a rhinoceros rushes from far south
of where I stand to charge the roast pig.

I sing louder and louder, echoing through the jungles.
The roast pig and the rhinoceros fight ferociously.
I sing till the rhino butts the roast pig in the air—
it lands on its back, legs straight up. When I wake, it's noon.

—October, 1977

ការផ្ទានដកស្ទូង

យប់ដកថ្ងៃស្ទូង ងើបអោនកោងៗ
ព្រលឹមព្រលប់ បនពតបង្ខំ
ដកស្ទូងអត់ឈប់ ព្រលឹមព្រលប់
គម្រប់ផែនការ ។

ម៉ែ អើយៗ ម៉ែ ស្ទូងស្រូវទល់ជ្រៃ
សុជន់ចុកផ្សា គ្មានសំរាកសោះ
កូនង៉ើតកូនង៉ា ស្រែកយំយ៉ាងណា
ម៉ែពុំបានឈប់ ។

"ទៅមួយហិតាទៀត!" អាភ្នែកភ្លើងស្រែក
"ឲ្យយើងទៅបំបៅកូនសិន" ម្ដាយទាំងឡាយសុំ ។
"កុំគិតកូនអី កុំភ័យ អង្គការមើលហើយ គិតតែស្ទូងទៅ!"

កូនខ្លីដាច់ពោះ ខ្លះងាប់ខ្លះរស់
ទាពេលព្រលប់ ពេលម៉ែមករក
កបដួនពេលយប់ ចំពេលកូនឈប់
ស្រែករកម៉ែហើយ ។

ម្ដាយបីកូនស្រែកយំទ្រហោ ៖
ឱកូនមាសម្ដាយកូនឃ្លានយ៉ាងណា ម៉ែជាទាសាចោលកូនដាច់ពោះ
មាសម្ដាយស្លាប់ទៅដោយដាច់ទឹកដោះ មិនគួរទេសោះអាទមិឡចង្រៃ ។
ធ្វើបាបកូនអញទាល់កូនអញងាប់ សុំកូនទៅប្រាប់យមរាជណាថ្ងៃ
ឲ្យជាក់ទោសាអាទមិឡចង្រៃ ឲ្យវាវរលាយរលត់កុំសល់ ។
ឱកូនមាសម្ដាយទៅទូលព្រះឥន្ទ បររថក្បៀរកិនបនពតព្រៃផ្សៃ
កំទេចបិសាចអសោចអប្រិយ៍ ស្រោចស្រង់កម្ពុជាជួបសុខសាន្តអើយ ។
កូន! កូន! កូនមាសម្ដាយ!

—មិថុនា-កញ្ញា ១៩៧៨

SEASON OF TRANSPLANTING RICE

At night, we uprooted young rice plants.
We transplanted them in the daytime,
bending our backs from 4:00 A.M. to 5:00 P.M.
No one understood the Red-Eyes' goal.

Mothers left their babies with the elder women.
The mothers' breasts were full of milk, causing pain
to the point of tears, while others had gone dry,
yet the Red-Eyes shouted, "Two more acres!"

The mothers said, "Let us go home to nurse our babies!"
But the Red-Eyes cut them off abruptly:
"Don't worry about them, get busy here!
Angkar has taken care of them already."

By evening, when the mothers were released,
some babies had starved to death, others were unconscious.
The only way the mothers bore this burden
was by raising a mournful wail:

"O, my child! My baby! How painfully you've suffered.
Because your mama is a slave—that's why you've left me.
May your spirit tell the King of Death to condemn the Red-Eyes,
to drive a magic chariot over these fields.

Baby! Baby! My dear baby!"

—June – September, 1978

អធិដ្ឋានពិសិដ្ឋ

1. ការដ្ឋានដាំដើម "គ" សំរោង ស្មូល ក្រចេះ

ឧសភាចិត្តប្រាំបី   អង្គការដាក់ទិសថ្មី
ឲ្យដាំដើម "គ"   ទាញយកសំឡី
ដូរយកគ្រាក់ទំរ   គំនិតពិតល្អ
       ទាស់អត់កំណើត ។

អង្គការជំកង់   និយាយត្រង់ៗ
ពីប្រជាជនថ្ម   "អង្គការដាក់ទិស
យកទៅប្រល័យ   ទាំងកូនក្នុងផ្ទៃ
       ដ៏ចោលឲ្យអស់
       នៅ ចិតសិបប្រាំបួន ខែ កុម្ភៈ ។"

ខ្ញុំតិតក្នុងចិត្ត   រន្ធត់អាណិត
ជនជាតិប្រុសស្រី   កើតនៅកម្ពុជា
អត់មានជីងអិ   ត្រូវវេទយក្ខិ
       ជាចំណីលេង ។

បណ្ដាំបិតា   "ពេលណាបុត្រា
មានទុក្ខធំធេង   បុត្រគោងឡូងស្តួង
បិតាចាត់ចែង   អេស្សរីណាត្រងង
       ជ្រោមជ្រែងផ្ដួយបុត្រ ។"

—ឧសភា ១៩៧៨

SACRED VOWS

for Michael Dennis Browne

I. KAPOK PLANTATION

May '78   /   Angkar puts out a new directive—
to grow kapok trees   /   to sell the fiber
in exchange for tractors.   /   It's a good dream
                        but it's impossible.

Angkar is sitting in a circle   /   talking openly
about the new people—   /   that "Angkar will set a plan in motion
to kill them off   /   even babies in the womb—
                    kill them off by February, '79."

I'm thinking to myself   /   that I feel pitifully frightened
for my people, men and women   /   who were born in Cambodia
and are naive about everything   /   —now comes the time when they
                    will be eaten by ogres.

I recollect my Father's words: /   "Whenever, son,
you face any great danger   /   you should pray
to Me for help!   /   I will assign your guru, Vesvorn,
                to help you, son, to save people."

                              —Samrong, Snoul, Kratie, May, 1978

II. អធិដ្ឋាន

ខ្ញុំជឿថា ខ្ញុំមិនអាចគេចផុតពីក្ដីស្លាប់បានឡើយ ។
ខ្ញុំចាំបណ្ដាំបារមីប្រាប់ថា ពេលមានទុក្ខធ្ងន់
ខ្ញុំត្រូវអុជធូបសំបូងសង្រ្គងសក្ដទេវរាជ
ជួយសង្រ្គោះជាតិប្រុសស្រី ។
ក្រោមពន្លឺចន្ទពេញវង់ ត្រង់ជាក់
ពេលយាមស្រួទុំការពារសគ្គព្រៃ
ខ្ញុំអុជធូប ២១ សរសដែលខ្ញុំបានធ្វើពីស្ទឹក គ
ហើយដោតចំលើក្បាលជំបុក —
ខ្ញុំសូត្រ នមោតស្ស ភគវតោ អរហតោ សម្មាសម្ពុទ្ធស្ស (បីចប់)

82

រូចសំបូងសង្រ្គង ៖
                    សូម

"ព្រះមហាព្រាហ្មា   ខ្ពស់លើសលោកា
ព្រះឥន្ទ្រកោសិយ   ព្រះមហាយ្យិកា
ព្រះមាតុព្រះបិ   ឥន្ទ្រនិម្មិតបុរី
          ខ្ញុំព្រះអង្គបួងសួង ។

មហាយ្យកោរាជផង   មហាយ្យកោសួស្ដ៍ហោង
បារមីទាំងពួង   បិតានាតនាយ
ជុំវិញជើងក្បួង   លើភ្នំក្នុងឈួង
          សមុទ្ទនានា ។

សូមជួយជេញទមិឡ្យ   អសុរមារចិត្តពាល
ពី កម្ពុជា   សូមសន្តិភាព
មានដល់ប្រជា   រូចជាអ្នកជា
          ជួបសិទ្ធិសេរី ។

II. PRONOUNCEMENT

I knew I could never escape. I remembered
what the Great Spirit had told me: in time of danger
I should burn incense and invoke Sakadevaraja, the King of Angels,
to save the lives of my countrymen and women.
Under the light of the full moon, while
guarding the rice paddy fields from marauding beasts,
I burned twenty-one sticks of incense I'd made from kapok leaves
and set them in a termite mound.

Then, three times, I recited:
"Namo tassa Bhagavato Arahato Samma Sambuddhassa."
Then I pronounced my Sacred Vows:

"O, God in His Highest Form,   /   higher than the Universe,
the King of Angels,   /   all the Great-Grandmother Deities,
my Mother and Father   /   on Heaven Island
                I pray to all of you.

Great-Grandfather Raja   /   Great-Grandfather Suos,
all the local deities,   /   King of the Sacred Cobra,
deities of the six directions,   /   deities of the mountains and the seas,
                bless these benedictions.

Drive the evil atheists,   /   those foolish devils,
out of Cambodia.   /   May Khmers
have peace!   /   May Khmers be emancipated!
                May Khmers be respected and free!

សូមជួយកំចាត់ សូមជួយបំបាត់
អសុរមារព្រៃផ្សៃ អោយវិនាសបង់
អស់ពីទឹកដី សូមប្រជាធិបតេយ្យ
មានដល់កម្ពុជា ។

កម្ពុជាឯករាជ្យ ប្រជាលែងខ្លាច
ខ្ញុំព្រះអង្គសច្ចា រាប់បាត្រថ្វាយបិ
ដកបណ្តាសា ពីកម្ពុជា
នាអង្គរវត្ត ។

សូមមហាឫកានាគ ព្រះថោងប្រត្យ័ក្ស
ជួយចាំសម្បថ ក្រោយជនតា
ឆ្លងវាលបីផុត ហែលផ្លូងរួចផុត
ប្រាកដតាមធមិ

ជនតានិមន្តសង្ឃ ជាងប្រាំរយអង្គ
សំដែងអភិធម្ម ជយន្តោជូនពរ
ប្រជានិករ ប្រសិទ្ធិពរ
កម្ពុជាធិបតី ។"

រាត្រីពេញបូណ៌រដូវកត្តឹក ខ្យល់បក់គគឹកកាត់ព្រៃស្មសាន
បក់ក្លិនស្រូវទុំកាត់យប់ស្ងាត់សូន្យ ពេលខ្ញុំបញ្ជូនសារថ្វាយបិតា ។
ផ្សែងធូបកង្កាញ់ត្របាញ់ទៅលើ ពីលើដំបូកឆ្ពោះទៅវេហាស៍
នាំ អធិដ្ឋានពិសិដ្ឋ ឆ្ពោះស្ថានព្រហ្ម នាពេលចន្ទ្រាចរឆ្ពោះបស្ចិម ។

—តុលា ១៩៧៨

Please banish all devils!   /   Please blow away
all supernatural devils   /   beyond the horizon!
Please scour Cambodia!   /   May democracy
         prevail in Cambodia!

When Cambodia is independent,   /   the people free from fears,
I promise to offer   /   alms to my fathers
at Angkor Wat   /   to lift the curse
         from Cambodia.

May my Great-Grandmother Cobra /   and the King of the Mountain Country
witness my Sacred Vows.   /   After I have crossed
these three wildernesses,   /   after I have reached
         the shore of genuine Freedom,

I will invite the monks   /   more than five hundred of them
to present Buddhist discourses,   /   to bless
all the people,   /   to celebrate
         the rebirth of my beloved Cambodia."

On the night of the full moon, October, '78
the moon shone brightly over the jungle
where the cold north wind
swept the rice paddy fragrance
through the silent midnight.

And from the top of a termite mound
the smokes of incense curled,
soaring to Heaven,
carrying my Sacred Vows to the Almighty
as the moon revolved westward.

                                     —October, 1978

កងត្រាចកងធ្មង់

I. ប្រផ្នូល
យប់ត្រជាក់ងងឹតឈឹង ។
សូរឈឺច្រត – តុក តុក តុក –
ដេរព័ន្ធជុំវិញខ្ញុំខ្ញុំ
បិដូចចោរហានេឃ្យើមកណ្ឋបយកការណ៍ ។

ញាំវរញ ញ្រើសហូ្ររជោក
ដោយហេរហាត់ លក់អត់ដឹងខ្លួន ។
បារមិខ្ញុំបប្រាប់ថាៈ
"កុំទៅណា ទ្រាំនៅតែមួយយប់
អ្នករំដោះមកដល់ហើយ!"

—យប់ទិ ១៧ វិច្ឆិកា ១៩៧៨ – ការដ្ឋានសំពោច

II. អាសាពិទិសប្ូពិ
ក្រោកពីដេកធ្លូរចិត្តខ្ជាក
ងាកឆ្មេងស្មាំក្រែងដូចយល់សប្ដិ
ពេលខ្ញុំរៀបចេញទៅភ្នំ ដុតជង
ផ្វរទឹក មកធ្វេចទ្ទ្ះបំភ្លើធ្វើការយប់ ។

ស្រាប់តែប្រធានអោងបាយរត់វិងចុះវិងឡើង
ពាសពេញការដ្ឋានបាយរូចស្រែកភ័យរន្ធត់ៈ
"កន្ទែងណានៅកន្ទែងហ្នឹង
យួនចូលហើយ! យួនចូលហើយ!"

រំពេចនោះ មិត២១ ពីរក្រុ្រឿងបោះព្ទ្យពីកេីតរ៉ើវ
ឆាបលើជំនានា –
ទម្លាក់ត្រាប់បែកប្រាំត្រាប់ ផ្ទុះរលើងដើមលើ
ផ្ទាច់ក្ប្ញាលអាប្រគខ្ទ ។

THE WHEEL TURNS

I. HARBINGER
In a cold dark night I hear
the *tock tock tock* of a shepherd's crook
around my shack; I thought it was
the Red-Eyes come to eavesdrop.

In a cold sweat, I held my breath, soaked to the skin.
When I fell asleep exhausted
my Guardian Spirit whispered:
"Stay here overnight;
the Liberator will arrive in due time."

—Sampoch Concentration Camp, night of November 17, 1978

II. MANNA FROM THE EAST
Woke up released, looked around, justifying my dream
while I got ready to go to the mountains;
up there they'd have me gather resin
for torches to light our night work.

Just then the field kitchen boss ran wild,
around and around, shouting:
"Stay right where you are!
Yuon coming! Yuon coming!"

Suddenly two MIG-21s swooped from the east
over the concentration camps.
Five bombs dropped, toppled trees,
clobbered some scoundrels.

ម៉េ! ម៉េ! ម៉េ! កុមារតប្រញាយ
ស្ទៀង ភ្ងង ចាស់ៗ ក្រាបស្រប៉ាបទៅនឹងជើ
ខ្ញុំត្រវិក្រមាទៅរក យន្តហោះ
ស៊ិញ៉ឲ្យទំលាក់ក្រាប់បេកទ្បេត ។

មិត២១ មួយអរលើក្បាលខ្ញុំ
ប៉ីង! ក្រាប់បេកផ្ទះ
ចម្ងាយហាសិបម៉េត្រពីខ្ញុំ
កំទេចក្រាប់បេកប៉ុនមេដៃខ្ចាតមកដល់ជើងខ្ញុំ ។

ខ្ញុំធើសអំបែងក្រាប់បង្ហាញអ្នកបើក មិត២១
"អរគុណលោកម្ចាស់យកអាសា!"
វិលត្រឡប់ទៅខ្មរកូ្ចន
ខ្ញុំដួលសន្លប់អត់ដឹងខ្លួ ។

—១៨ វិច្ឆិកា ១៩៧៨

III. បេកសំបុក

ពួកចោរហានឈឺស្ងាយ អាកា ចិន
ឈរអោមខ្មខ្ញុំជិតហើយស្រែកៈ
"រៀបអីវ៉ាន់លឿនឡើង ទៅភ្ជំុជី"
ខ្ញុំឮ្ញល្ងើយៗ បើកភ្នែកស្ទើរមិនរួច ។

ខ្ញុំក្រនក្តៅ ក្តៅខ្លាំងគ្មានចង់ទៅណាទេ
តែអាចោរក្បួរយើងឲ្យចេញមុនថ្ងៃលិច
ខ្ញុំផ្ទកអីវ៉ាន់ តាយាយមូលដ្ឋានលើរទេះគោ
បររទេះទៅទិសឧត្តរ ក្រោមព្រះចន្ទពេញវង់ ។

"Ma! Ma! Ma!"—children stampeded.
Old Stiengs and Phnongs fell prostrate on the ground
I squinted at the MIGs, waving my *krama,*
signalling the pilots to drop some more.

A MIG veered back.
Booknn! another bomb exploded
fifty meters east of me
and a piece of shrapnel rolled to my feet.

Picked it up—
"Thanks, Liberator!" I held it up for the pilots to see.
Scrambling back to the shack to check on my son,
I fell down unconscious.

—November 18, 1978

III. DISPERSAL
Swarms of Red-Eyes with AK-47s
stood around my shack shouting
"Pack stuff for Phnom Chi!"
Half understanding, I hardly opened my eyes.

I was sick, too sick to go anywhere,
but the Red-Eyes forced us to leave before sunset.
I loaded an oxcart with the elderly and their gear—
we were herded northward while the moon rose like a disk of cheese.

មនុស្សប្រសេចប្រសាចពីគ្រប់ទិសទី
ប្រជ្រៀតគ្នាតែផ្លូវមួយ – ឆ្ពោះភ្នំជី
ទាំងរន្ធត់ ខ្ញុំបវរទេៅជាមួយគេ
ក្តុតជំទិងបណ្ឌើរ – ភ្លេចអស់ពាក្យបណ្ដាំបារមី ។
ពុទ្ធោ កម្មអីខ្ញុំ!

មេម៉ាយប្រជាជនថ្មីម្នាក់ ត្រូវរបួសធ្ងន់
ត្រង់ថ្ពាល់ឆ្អេង អង្គុយឲ្យខ្ញុំជិកគាត់
ទេៅជំរះស្រែក្រៅ តែសភាវគតិខ្ញុំមិនព្រម:
"បជិសេធទេៅ! កុំយកអាសាស្រ្តី-កុំផ្សៀសំជីប្រុស!"

ខ្ញុំមិនអើពើនឹងអង្គរករគាត់ទេ តែចិត្តអាណោចក្រៃ
ហើយជម្មើក្ដៅខ្ញុំកាន់តែខ្លាំងផង
អាចារបាទេឃ្យៀបញ្ជាប់ក្បួនរទេៅ
ខ្ញុំជេកនឹងជី ក្តុតជំទិង ជ្វាត្មងពេញមួយយប់តែម្តង ។

ពេលខ្ញុំផ្ដួបអ្នកស្រីនោះនៅភ្នំពេញ – ឆ្នាំ១៩៨៥
គាត់ថាទាំំជោះសង្គ្រោះគាត់
ពេលរទេៅខ្ញុំចេញផុតទេៅក្នុងព្រៃបន្ទិច
មុនថ្ងៃរះ – កម្មអើយ!

✻ ✻

នេះគីព្រោះតែភ្លាត់មាត់ ។ – ថ្ងៃមួយពេលឡេីងពីស្ទុង
ទាសករ កម្មោះ ក្រមុំ ជេីរក្បៀកខ្ញុំសួរថា ៖
"តា តា កាលណាបានយេីងួចទេៅស តា?"
"ជិតហេីយចៅ នៅពីរបីខែទេៀតទេ! ត្រាំទេៅចៅ!"

Tributaries of people from all directions
converged into one river—headed to Phnom Chi.
Absorbed by fear, I drove the oxcart in among others,
vomiting along the way, forgetting the words of the Spirit.
What karma I had to bear!

A woman, one of the new people, with a deep wound
on her left cheek, begged me to transport her
to Sre Krao Camp, but my instincts warned me:
"Deny her—don't befriend the woman."

I ignored her pleas, though my heart was breaking.
And my fever began to rise.
Then the Red-Eyes called the column to a halt.
I lay on the ground, throwing up all night.

I met that woman again in Phnom Penh, in '85—
she told me that Vietnamese troops had rescued her
after we'd been herded into the thick of the woods
just before dawn of the next day.

                    ✖ ✖

This is what happened because of a slip of my tongue:
One day after we'd been transplanting rice,
young slave men and women approached me and asked,
"Old man, old man, when will we be free?"

កម្លោះខ្លះថា ៖ "បើពិតមែន ខ្ញុំនឹងស៊ុពទាកូនឱាយផ្លែត!"
ខ្លះថា ៖ "អញស៊ុតុចទារវិញ!" ឯស្រី១ ថា ៖
"អញធ្វើជាប្រពន្ធចុងរបស់លោកណាក៏ធ្វើដែរ
នៅជាទាសករដូចនេះមិនដឹងជាប់ថ្ងៃណាទេ!"

ខ្ញុំថា ៖ "ដល់ពេលនោះ ខ្ញុំត្រូវទៅថ្វាយបង្គំ
ម្ចាស់បង ក្រពុំឈូក នៅវិហារ
សសរម្មួយរយងសម្បុណិសិន
ទើបខ្ញុំទៅភ្នំពេញ ។

—ល្ងាចទី ១៩ វិច្ឆិកា' ១៩៧៨

92 |

IV. ដំណើរឆ្លោះភ្នំជី
ភ័យខ្លាចទ័ព័ដេរាះដេញទាន់
អាហារនេយ៉ូបញ្ហាយើងឲ្យចូលពួនក្នុងព្រៃជាញ្ជាយ
រយៈពិរអាទិត្យតាមផ្លូវទៅភ្នំជី
ជម្លើខ្ញុំមិនអន់ថយសោះ ។

ឧសថតែម្យ៉ាងខ្ញុំអាចរកបានគឺស្លឹកស្ពៅ
ចង់ជាធាប់ ខ្ញុំទំពារលេបផ្ដលបណ្ដាលឲ្យក្អួតជាំទឹង
អាមេហានេយ៉ូគំរាមថា៖ "មិនប្រឹងឲ្យជាធាប់
ប្រយ័ត្នទុកកន្លែងហ្នឹង តា ឯង!"

ភ្នែកខ្ញុំស្រវាំងកាន់តែខ្លាំង
ខ្ញុំសម្ឹងមើលកូន – ឃើញកូនប៉ុនកន្លាត
ខ្ញុំប្រឹងភាវនារំពឹក "អធិដ្ឋានពិសិដ្ឋ
សច្ចាប្រណិធាន ពេល ខ្ញុំដេកផ្ងារ មើលមេឃ ។

I said, "It's almost time, grandchildren—
two or three more months—be patient."
One young man said, "When it happens, I will stuff
my stomach with fetus duck eggs."

Another said "I will gorge myself on noodles!"
A young woman said, "I'd rather be the tenth wife of any petty bigshot
than remain a slave, knowing death may come at any moment."
Without thinking, I tried to one-up them:

"When that time comes, before heading home to Phnom Penh,
I will go to visit my Princess Krabum Chhouk
at the Hundred-Column Temple at Sambor,"
little knowing that this would actually come to pass.

—evening, November 18, 1978

IV. JOURNEY TO PHNOM CHI
Terrified of the v/n troops,
the Red-Eyes repeatedly ordered us to hide in the woods.
Two weeks on the trails to Phnom Chi, and my fever
never abated.

My only medicine—neem leaves.
To speed my recovery, I chewed too many,
turning my stomach inside out.
The Red-Eyes passed by saying: "Sick, Ta?—try to get well . . .
if not, we'll have to leave you here."

My vision was blurred.
I gazed at my son—he was small as a bug.
I tried to recall my Sacred Vows,
my Oath of Allegiance, while I lay face up to the sky.

ប្រឹងសម្លឹងព្រះអាទិត្យ
ថ្ងៃឡើងស្រអាប់ ដូចពពកបាំង
ខ្ញុំស្ងើររហើបមាត់មិនរួចនឹងនិយាយថាៈ
"ឱ ព្រះឥន្ទ្រកោសិយ ខ្ញុំព្រះអង្គកំពុងងាប់ហើយ!

សូមប្រទានពរឲ្យបុត្រនៅមានអាយុផង!
រស់ចាំប្រាប់លោកថាពិតជាមានព្រះមែន
ព្រះផ្តល់យុត្តិធមិ
ដល់អ្នកមានជំនឿលើព្រះអង្គ ។"

អាហានេយ្យធ្លាក់យករទេះពីខ្ញុំ ឲ្យខ្ញុំតគេះគគ្រតៈតាមវា
ដល់ខ្លួនភ្ញាក់កណ្តាលស្មូសាន វាឈប់សំរាក
អធ្រាត្រក្នុងសុបិន ខ្ញុំឃើញទេវតាទ្រង់ស្មៀ ស ពីរអង្គ
ឈរញញឹមដាក់ខ្ញុំ – ពេលខ្ញុំប្រកាច់ – ត្រឹកឡើងជម្មុធ្លុរស្រាក ។

v. ជំរំស្រែប្រាំរយ
បានសេចក្តីប្រោសពីព្រះ ខ្ញុំជើររេ្វតេ្រទាតទៅឲ្យត
ឆ្លងព្រែក ជើរកាត់កោះ
ទៅដល់ជំរំស្រែប្រាំរយ ។
មនុស្សកកកុញ្ញមកពីគ្រប់ទិសទី
ត្រូវបង្ខំឲ្យច្រូត ៤០ កណ្ដាប់ម្នាក់ក្នុងមួយថ្ងៃ
ស៊ីតែបបរ និង ជំទ្បួងដដែល ។
វេលាម៉ោងដប់យប់
អាចារបហានេយ្យបណ្តើរមនុស្ស ២០០ នាក់
កណ្ដាលខែភ្លើ យកទៅប្រហារចោល
"តា ហ្លោល គោះ ទៅជាមួយយើង!" ម្នាក់ស្តាល់ខ្ញុំស្រែកឡើង
"ខ្ញុំសុខចិត្តហុតបបរ មិនទៅជាមួយបងទេ!"

I stared at the sun.
The sun was dark, as if there were clouds
in front of it. I hardly opened my mouth
to say "O, Preah Indra Kosei, I'm dying!

May I be spared to live on,
to show the world that there really is the Almighty
who renders justice to those
who believe in Thee!"

The oxcart taken from me, I staggered along behind others.
In the night, somewhere on a mound in the jungle,
my sickness at the point of climax, two beautiful girls
in white veils smiled at me: my fever broke.

V. FIVE HUNDRED RICE PADDY CAMP
Begging mercy from God, I staggered forward.
Crossing rivers, across islands,
we reached the Five Hundred Rice Paddy Camp;
an infestation of people from everywhere
forced to harvest forty sheaves each a day
with almost no rice for they themselves to eat.
One night at 10:00 P.M., 200 innocents
were escorted from their jobs
to a mass grave in the moonlight.
"Ta Gold, go with us!" one acquaintance called to me.
"No, I'd rather take gruel than leave with you."
Only abandoned shanties left behind. My family had to move,
to keep up with the Red-Eyes. Still the Red-Eyes
tried to clear the forest to be corn fields.

ផ្ទះទាំងឡាយក្លាយជាអាស្រមខ្មោច ។ គ្រួសារខ្ញុំត្រូវរើទៅទៀត
តាមអាហានេយ្យំប្រឆ្វំ ។ សភាពការណ៍ម៉្លឹងហើយ
ពួកវានៅតែឆ្មៀតរានព្រៃជាចំការពោតទៀត
ខ្ញុំឈឺទៀត – ចាញ់ព្រែក កំពី ។ ស្វាត់ឈឹង –
ចាបក៏លែងយំ ចង្រិតក៏ឈប់ស្រែក ។

ឯកោនៅក្នុងខ្ទមពេទ្យ – ចាំមច្ចុរាជ
ក៏ព្រោះតែបារមី "អធិដ្ឋានពិសិដ្ឋ"
មានក្មេងម្នាក់បររទេះគោ
ទៅដឹកខ្ញុំឲ្យជុំគ្រួសារវិញ ។

vi. នៅច្រាំងទន្លេមេកុង ខេត្ត កំពង់ធំ
ដំណើរឆ្ពោះភ្នំដី ប្រព្រឹត្តទៅទៀត ។
ខ្សោយខ្លាំង ពាក់កណ្ដាលខ្មោច ខ្ញុំដេកនៅមាត់ច្រាំង
អាហានេយ្យំក៏ឈប់ចែកអង្ករឲ្យគ្រួសារខ្ញុំទៀត ។
ជិតភ្លឺ អនុជត្រី ពិដោររមានឫទ្ធិ ខ្សឹបប្រាប់ថា៖
"ភ័យអីទៀត ភ្នំពេញរំដោះហើយ!"

—ទី ១១ មករា ១៩៧៩

ខ្ញុំអង្វរអាហានេយ្យំសុំងាប់នៅច្រាំងទន្លេត្រូវបដិសេធ
ក្រុមវាលើកខ្ញុំដាក់លើរទេះទៅភ្នំដីទៀត
ធ្វើដំណើរអស់មួយថ្ងៃ គេឈប់សំរាក
សំឡេះគោចែកសាច់គ្នា អត់តែគ្រួសារខ្ញុំ ។

កូនខ្ញុំរើសឆ្អឹងជើងមុខបានពីរ
កូនខ្ញុំសប្បាយណាស់-ពេលយប់វាដុតជើងគោ
"ឪ ស្អែកយើងបានស៊ុបគោហើយមែនទេ?"
"មែនកូន!" ជលនេត្រខ្ញុំហូរច្រោក ។

—ទី ១២ មករា ១៩៧៩

I fell ill again. Very quiet,
not a song from the birds, no chirring insects—
alone at a shack in the jungle, waiting for Death.
But I remained in the shadow of my Sacred Vows;
a boy with an oxcart carried me to my family.

VI. MEKONG RIVERBANK, KOMPONG THOM PROVINCE
Again we started forward to Phnom Chi.
Lying half dead on the far bank of the fourth river,
when the Red-Eyes refused to distribute pestled rice to me,
my Invisible Sister,Pido Mean Roeudhi, told my wife
Phnom Penh had been liberated.

—January 11, 1979

My plea to die on the bank rejected,
the Red-Eyes loaded me on an oxcart to Phnom Chi again.
After one day's journey, they rested in the rice fields.
They slaughtered cattle and shared meat.

But not with my family. My boy scavenged two front leg bones.
My boy was happy; that night he scorched the hooves.
"Dad, tomorrow we will have soup . . . ha!"
"Yes, son," I half-answered.

—January 12, 1979

ដំណើររទេះភ្លើងត្រូវសំរាកទ្បេរត ។ អាហារនេឃ្យៀចាត់
ពួកឈ្មួបឡ្យទៅមើលតើទំរំដោះដល់ណាហើយ ។
"ឱ! សុ៎បឆ្ងិនហើយ – ម៉ាហ្ស៊ុបសុ៎ប ឱ!"
ខ្ញុំរារទៅរកឆ្ងាងសុ៎ប ។
ស្រាប់តែដ៏រផ្ដើលជាន់គោ
គោប្រាសបោលទាត់ខ្លាយសុ៎បអស់ខានសុ៎
កំភ្លើង អាកាចិត របការ៎ង៎ ចោលគររទៅគល់លើ
រទេះ សត្វពាហនៈបាត់ម្ចាស់អស់ ។
អាចារហានេឃ្យៀគេចបាត់ឈឹង ដួចផ្ទ្បេងបារី
អត់ទាំងបាយ អស់ទាំងសុ៎ប ។

—ទី ១៣ មករា ១៩៧៩—

VII. ត្រឡប់វិលរកផ្ទះ
ត្រឡប់ក្រោយរង្វេងបាត់ទិស សំណាងល្អ ជួប អតីតសក្ដិប៊ី
ខ្ញុំជួនគេ ក្រដាស់ម្ដៃដុល្លា ភ្ស៊ិយឈេស ដែលម្ចាយខ្ញុំលាក់ក្នុងខោទ្រនាប់គាត់ ។
គេជួយចម្ងងនឹងក្បូនដាក់វិហារ –
សសរម្ចួយរបរ ស្រុកសំបូណិ ៌ខេត្តក្រចេះ ដួចខ្ញុំបាន "ភ្លាត់មាត់"

យើងស្ងាក់នៅលើផ្ទះមួយធំ
ឃ្យានស្ងើរដោប់ពោះ – ខ្ញុំប្រឹងគ្ថេះគ៎ះទៅរកត្រី
ផ្ទកម្ចួយទឹកត្រីមជ្ឈុង
មានត្រីមាត់ផ្ទុចចុះ ផ្ទចទ្បេ៎ង ដួចច្រើនណាស់ ។

ខ្ញុំចាប់បាចនឹងទ្រនាប់ជើងកង់ទ្បាន
បាច បាច ពីព្រឹក ទល់ ត្រង់ទើបវិង
កាយភក់រកត្រី តែកំភ្លាញមួយ ក៏គ្មាន ផង
"ឱ ម្ចាស់បង ក្រពុំលួក ឆើយ សុ៎ត្រីមួយ ម៉ោ!"

Mid-morning on the road to Phnom Chi, they rested.
The Red-Eyes went to scout for V/N up ahead.
"Dad, the soup is ready. Come, Dad!" I was weak
but I crawled toward the soup.
Suddenly cattle rampaged everywhere—
Not the soup!
AK-47S, B-40S, ammunition pitched in the trees,
oxcarts, cattle left behind;
all traces of the Red-Eyes had vanished like smoke—
even the rice from the spilled soup.

—January 13, 1979

VII. RETURNING HOME
Wandering back, I met an ex-captain. I gave him
a U.S. twenty-dollar bill my mother had hidden in her vagina.
By bamboo raft, he sailed us to the tomb—the Hundred-Column Temple,
Sambor—fulfilling the slip of my tongue.

We squatted at an abandoned house.
Starving to death, I staggered out to look for fish.
A pond with water up to my knees
was full of bubbling carp.

I splashed the water out of the pond with a slipper.
This bailing was interminable.
And then there was not a single fish in it.
I sighed "O, Princess Lotus Bud, give me a fish!"

អស់សង្ឃឹម ពីរនាក់ ឱ-កូន ត្រឡប់ទៅជម្រកវិញ
ថ្វេភ្លោ៎ហេង ជីក្រៀមចេស –
បែកក្រហែង
ខ្ញុំខ្ងេះរកកដ្ងេបស្រួតាមក្រហែងជីស្រែ ។

ក្បាលត្រីផ្ដក់លេចចេញ
ពីជើងក្នុងកូនក្រែងគោកមួយ
"ខ្ញោចលងឬកូន!"
"ត្រីតេី ឱ!" កូនខ្ញុំឆ្លើយ ។

យើងល្ងៀង អាហារក្រង់ យ៉ាងឆ្ងាញ់
មានកម្ទាំង យើងទៅចេតិយម្ទាស់បង ក្រពុំឈ្ងុក
ថ្ងាយផ្ទាឈ្ងុក អុជទ្យៀន១គូ ធួបម្ទេម្ទួយសរវ័ស
ស្ត្រ នមោ បិចប់ ។
ខ្ញុំថ្ងេងវាចា ៖

ម្ទាស់បង ក្រពុំឈ្ងុក កំពូលភព!
អនុជសន្យាថាមកគោរពម្ទាស់បង
ឥឡូវខ្ញុំម្ទាស់មកមែន! សូមម្ទាស់បង
ជួយជួនដំណើរទៅផ្ងះប្រកបដោយសុវត្ថិភាពផង!

សូមមានអ្នកយកឥាសាខ្ញុំម្ទាស់តាមផ្ងវផង!
សូមទឹកជីយើងមានសេរីភាព ប្រជាជនយើងជួបតែសុខ!
សូមគោរពម្ទាស់បង!
សូមអ្នកធំគោរពសិទ្ធិមនុស្សកុំបីខានទ្យេីយ!

បើខ្ញុំម្ទាស់ជាបុគ្គលឥតប្រយោជន៍សំរាប់ទឹកជីយើង
សូមម្ទាស់បងបំបរបង់ខ្ញុំម្ទាស់ចុះ ។
ម្ទាស់បង! ម្ទាស់ស្ត្រី!
ទុកឱ្យខ្ញុំម្ទាស់សូន្យទៅ សូន្យទៅ រហូតលត់សង្ខារទៅចុះ ។"

Beyond hope, I returned to the shelter.
The sun was blistering hot,
the earth was parched and cracked.
I searched for rice-frogs in the cracks.

A big round carp head
stuck out of the drying mud
in a dry pond. "Is it a spook, son?"
I asked. "No, it is a fish, Dad!" my boy responded.

We enjoyed a big meal that day.
Feeling restored, we went to Princess Krabum Chhouk's tomb.
I burned nine sticks of incense, reciting,
"Namo tassa Bhagavato Arahato Samma Sambuddhassa."
(three times)

Then I intoned:
"Praise be to you, my Princess Krabum Chhouk!
I pledged to come, now I'm here in front of you.
May my journey home be safe;

May someone befriend me on the way;
may our land be free; and may our people be happy.
Praise be to You, Machah Bong!
May Human Rights be respected!

"If my lot is to be of no use to this land of ours,
may Machah Bong expel me from this land.
Praise be to You, Princess Sister!
Let me dwindle away for as long as my life may last."

ពេលថ្ងៃគងត្រា ខ្ញុំអង្គុយសម្លឹងមើលទឹកកួច
ស្ទើចកន្ទោងវាស្ទានាម្ចាស់បង វគនមាលី
ច្រាសទឹកមកដល់ទីនេះ ។
ងមេយឡើងក្រហមឆ្នោងនាយព្រាំខ្យេរវិនស្មឹកឈើ ។

បក្ស្រាបក្ស៊ីហើរឆ្លាត់ផ្ទែង
ទៅមករក្សទន់
"ឱ កម្ពុជា អើយ!
មានតែការជះៈជាន់ញាំញីច្រើនឆ្នាំតទ្បេត!"

102 |

"ប៉ុន្ថែ យើងរួចពីក្រញាំខ្លា ហើយកូន!
គោៈទៅផ្ងូៈយើង កូន!
គេរំដោៈយើងហើយ!
យើងសេរីហើយ! សេរី! សេរី!

គោៈយើងទៅ! ទៅ! ទៅ!
គោៈយើងបេៈផលាញ្ញាំ!
គោៈយើងបេៈបន្ទែស្ច!
គោៈយើងចាប់ត្រី – អើសយកអាធំៗ

គោៈយើងដាំស្ច! គោៈយើងញ្ញាំ! គោៈយើងដេក!
គោៈយើងមុជទឹក! គោៈយើងហែលលេង កូន!
ហែលទៅរកសេរីភាព!
សេរីភាព កូន! សេរីភាព!"

—១៤ មករា ១៩៧៩—

In the evening, sitting with my face to the sunset
I contemplated a whirlpool in the river,
wondering how fate had brought my Princess to this spot,
while beyond the lush forest, the horizon was crimson.

The forest birds flew free
to and fro from their nests.
"O, Cambodia,
only to be trampled for many years to come!"

"But we are free from tigers, son!
Let's go home, son! We are liberated!
We are free! Free! Free! Free!
Let's go! Go! Go! Go!

Let's pick wild fruit;
let's pick wild vegetables;
let's fish, catch fish—choose the biggest one.
Let's cook! Let's eat! Let's sleep.

Let's dive into the water;
let's take a swim, son—
swim to Freedom!
Freedom, son! Freedom!"

—January 14, 1979

ឡប់ស្មារតី

រាត្រីនោះត្រជាក់មែន
ខ្ញុំដុតភ្លើងកំដៅ
សូរគោះទ្វារ ៖ តុក – តុក – តុក!
"ស្អី អ្នកណាគោះទ្វារ?" ខ្ញុំស្រែកឡើង ។

"បើកទ្វារ! ឬអញបាញ់ទម្លាយឥឡូវ!" សម្លេងសន្ធាប់ពីក្រៅ
ខ្ញុំញាំរួចចកដ្បូចត្រូវអំបិល
ខ្ញុំបើកទ្វារ ខ្មែរក្រហមម្នាក់ចូលមក
កាំភ្លើងនៅដៃភ្ជង់ចំខ្ញុំ ។

"អ្នកណាឱ្យដុតភ្លើងលើផ្ទះ?
ស្អែកចេញពីនេះ ឬអញបាញ់ចោល"
ពុទ្ធោ កម្មអ៊ី !
កាលណាទៅទៀបជួបសុខ?

ព្រហាមស្រាងៗយើងចេញពីវិហារសសរ ១០០
វែក ទួលកម្មសិទ្ធិចក្ខុច
ដើរគេះគេះយឺតៗ ។ កន្ទែងណាក៏ជាផ្ទះ
យើងដើរពីរបីគីឡូម៉ែត្រឈប់ម្ដង ។

យើងទៅស្ងូចត្រឹងទន្លេមេកុង
តែអត់ដែលបានត្រីទេ ។ សំណាងល្អ
ប្រទះបានក្បាលគោមួយ
យើងយកមកប្រឡោះយកសាច់ – ស្ងោរស៊ុប – ឆ្លាញ់មែន ។

ព្រលប់កាលណា យើងធ្វើដំណើរទៀត
ខ្ញុំទួលក្បាលគោទុកស៊ីស្អែកទៀត
យប់យន់ យើងឈប់ដេកលើផ្ទះមួយ
គ្មានអ្នកណាហ៊ានទៅក្បែរផ្ទះនោះទេ ។

DISORIENTATION

That night it was so cold
that I started a fire to warm us.
Pok! Pok! Pok! on the door.
"What the hell, who dares knock on the door?" I shouted.

"Open the door, or I'll shoot it off the hinges!" a voice screamed.
I quivered like a skinned frog dipped in salt.
I opened the door. A Khmer Rouge came in
with a gun pointed at me.

Who gave you permission to light this fire?
Tomorrow you'd better leave,
or you'll all be executed."
O, Kamma! When shall I be free of this?

The next morning we left the Hundred-Column Temple.
Balancing our bundle of possessions on my head,
I stumbled slowly along the road. Wherever we stopped
was our home—we stopped every two or three miles.

For food, I went fishing in the Mekong River,
with a line and one hook. I caught no fish, of course.
Instead I found a cow's head left over from slaughtering.
We cut off the flesh and made soup—yes, good soup!

It was dark then, so we had to move on.
I carried the rest of the cow's head along with us.
We spent the night in an abandoned house,
and for some reason, everyone steered clear of us.

ព្រហាមឡេ្យីង គេនិយាយថា
ផ្ទះខ្លាចគេី! ម្មេចហ៊ានជេក
វាហ្ស៊ូសទៅហេី៍យ
ខ្ញុំនេ៎ងជាខ្លាចដេីរនោះ ។

"ខ្ួរគោធ្លាញ់ណាស់!" ខ្ញុំប្រាប់កូន
"ហ្ឌឹងហេី៍យ ធេិ៍មេ៍ចយកខ្ួរបាន?"
ម្នាក់ៗសំឡ្ឌឹងខ្ញុំ ហ្ូរហេ៍តាមផ្ួរ
ខ្ញុំភ្ាក់ខ្ួន "ឆ្ុតអ៊ីទៅទ្ុលឆ្ឌឹងក្ឌាលគោ ។"

ខ្ញុំបោះឆ្ឌឹងក្ឌាលគោចោល
ខ្ញុំទៅបេ៎ះបន្ទេតាមបឹង – ដកក្រឌិឡ្ួក
សុំទានប្រហុកអ្នកស្រុកបានបីកន្ុយ
ហេី៍យយេ៍ឯងស៊ីបា៍យឆ្ាញ់ដដេល ។

មនុស្សបរទេ៎ះខ្លាន់ខ្លាប់
គេ៎ពីរបី៍ថ្ៃថ្ៃបា៍ត់ស្ឈា៍ត់ឈ៍ឍង
យេ៍ឯងឆ្ើ៍ដំណេីរឯកឯង-ខ្ញុំឆ្ើរទេ៎អ្ួស –
ឆ្ុកអ៎ង្ឝរ បា៍នឆ្ឆ្ាំឯលេីរទេ៎ ។

ដល់ស្រុក សំបុក អាឈ្ួនម្នាក់ចេ៎ញៃនក
រុកធី វារ៎ខ្ួនខ្ញុំ វិ៍បអ្ួសយក
បា៍កា ប៎័រ៎កែរ ៥១ ស្ាស៎ សំណល់កេ៎រពីអា៍មេ៍រិក
ហ្ូស៎ពិ៍ភ៍យ ខ្ញុំស៎ួរវា៎ះ កក ក៍ីម ខ៎ង?

មា៍នបា៍យទេ៎?
ទាហា៍នម្នាក់យកបា៍យមួ៎យជុ៎ំហ្ុចឲ្យ៎ខ្ញុំ
"កំអ៎៍ីន! អរគុ៎ណា៍!"
និ៍យាយឈ្ួនកុ៎ំឲ្យវា៍ៃឆ្កឈួរ ។

In the morning, the others told us
that the house was inhabited by spooks.
It was too late for me to be afraid of ghosts—
I was a walking ghost myself.

"Cow brains are good!" I told my boy.
"Yes, but how can we get them out of there?"
Everyone looked at me as we walked along.
I sensed that they wondered why I was

balancing the cow's head on my own, so I pitched it.
We picked wild vegetables, dug roots.
I begged three small salted fish from the base people.
And we enjoyed our meal just the same.

Hordes of people everywhere, but they all drove oxcarts.
In a few days everyone had disappeared.
We were alone. I then made a two-wheeled cart.
I towed the cart with our puny "luggage" on it.

A Yuon emerged from the woods.
He searched my body, our bags, at gunpoint.
He robbed the few remaining keepsakes I'd saved from the u.s.
Beyond fear, I asked him: "Co coeum khong?

Toi sin coeum ma chuck?"
Another soldier gave me a crust of cold rice.
"Cam oeun, thank you!"
We continued our trip.

បាក់រស្យេលយើងមកដល់ក្រុងក្រចេះ
យើងតាំងទិកណ្ដាលវាលស្រែ –
ដំបាយអាស្រ័យ រួចដេកស្រណោះខ្លន
មិនគួរខកប្រាណាមកពីស្នេហាជាតិស្មោះ ។

ដេរចុះ ដេររឭងផ្លូប នុត ដារ៉ា
ដែគ្ធាក់ទិកទៅ បុះ លារ
គាត់ហៅខ្ញុំទៅទៅជាមួយ
ខ្ញុំបានធូរបន្តិច មានសាច់អាស្រ័យខ្លះ ។

គួច គ្រដេក (ម្រេញគង្វាល)
សណ្ឋិតកូន នុត ដារ៉ា
បង្ខំយាយ ប្រេះ សារុន ឱ្យប្រញាប់
ទៅភ្នំពេញ ពុំនោះទៅខ្មែរក្រហមក្បេររទៅវិញ ។

—ខែ កុម្ភ: ១៩៧៩

ខ្លាចខ្មែរក្រហម-ក្រុមយើងមកកភ្នំពេញ
នុត ដារ៉ាសុខចិត្តយកអាសាខ្ញុំទាំងទេិសទាល់
ដល់ បុះ លារ ខ្មយើងផ្ងាប់នៅ
ទិកឡ្យើងបោសបាត់អស់ ។

ដល់ជំរំវ្រៃព្រែក តា អាំ
យើងចូលមើលមុខផ្ងបសម្ងាប់កូនភ្លោះខ្ញុំ
ខ្ញុំគ្ខានចិត្តកុំកូនទាល់តែសោះ
ខ្ញុំប្រិងញញឹមដាក់គេ ហើយដេររទៅទ្យេត ។

ដល់វគ្តព្រៃព្រែកដំបូក ខ្ញុំឈ័ខ្លាំង
រហូតដល់ភ្លឺក ។
យប់នោះគោ នុត ដារ៉ា មួយប្រកាច់
ដួលគឹងដាប់ក្បែររខ្ញុំ ។ ខ្ញុំធូរខ្យាក ។

We arrived at Kracheh in the late afternoon,
set up camp under the open sky,
and prepared dinner.
In the morning, an ex-professor called on me.

He asked us to stay in his house with him.
And the next day, Nuth Dara,
my ex-partner at the concentration camp,
invited us to stay with him.

Not for long, though, as Toch the elf, who had followed me,
possessed Dara's daughter and urged us
to reach Phnom Penh as soon as possible:
"If not, the Khmer Rouge will return, and you'll be captured again."

—February, 1979

Terrified of the Khmer Rouge, the group set out for Phnom Penh.
Nuth Dara befriended me at first because of Toch.
We passed by the second concentration camp—
not a single shack remained.

At the first concentration camp
we called on one of the women who had killed my twins,
but I was too weak to take revenge.
I tried to smile at her, but just walked past.

At Wat Prek Dambok, I became sick again,
falling into a swoon. A healthy bull standing next to me
fell dead; my sickness broke.
When they slaughtered it, I asked for some of the liver.

គេឲ្យធ្វើគោបធ្លិច ខ្ញុំសូញ្ចាំក្នាម វំពេចនោះខ្ញុំយឺឡ្យេត
អឃ្យកោសូស្ស្តីបន្ទូលថា គាេនោះលោកដួរនឹងជីវិតខ្ញុំ
ស៊ីសាច់គោដូចស៊ុសាច់ឯង បានជាឈឺ ពេលខ្ញុំផ្ទួបអឃ្យកោ
ជាវា ឈប់យកអាសាខ្ញុំហើយ ។

យើងត្រូវផ្ទួលរទេះ អ៊ិង
ឲ្យម្ចាយក្មេកនិងកូនខ្ញុំជិះ
ដល់ អផៃញ្ចង ពុកបូស្ស៊ី
ខ្ញុំផ្ញាក់ខួនដល់វារផៃលេងរច ។

ខ្ញុំទៅជាខ្លាចទៅហើយ –
មើលមិនឃើញ ស្តាប់មិនឮ
ប្រពន្ធខ្ញុំញុថា អង្គភឹម ចូលគេ
ក៏ប្រាសទៅសុំទឹកមួយកន្ទោងស៊ីកឈ្យក ។

ប្រពន្ធខ្ញុំបណ្តក់ទឹកដាក់មាត់ខ្ញុំ
លុបមុខឲ្យខ្ញុំ ។ ព្រឹកឡ្យើងស្វាងចែស
យើងបណ្តដំណើរ – ដល់រត្តខ្លក ត្រីយខាងកើតភ្នំពេញ
យើងស្មោរមាន់ផៃសនអ្នកតា

សុំផ្សរចូលផ្ងះកំណឹតកូនវិញ
យើ៎ងទៅដល់ផ្ងះច្បារអំពៅ
នៅកណ្ឋាលខែ កុម្ភៈ ១៩៧៩
ផ្ងះខ្ញុំទៅសល់ផៃតសំបក – បាត់ស្យេវភៅអស់ ។

When I ate it, I fell sick again. Later, my Grandpa Suos
told me that Dara's bull had passed away on my behalf;
I'd gotten sick, then, from eating my own flesh!
But Dara used it as an excuse to leave us behind.

We hired an oxcart belonging to Ong,
just to carry rice and my mother-in-law.
At Anhjeng Pouk Roeussei, I couldn't
even crawl, nor could I speak.

Lying still on the ground, like a corpse,
I could see nothing, hear nothing.
Grandpa Ang Phim possessed a medium who gave
medicine to my wife in a lotus leaf.

She washed my face with it, dripped some into my mouth.
I came alive, and in the morning we continued our trip
to Khokhpok Pagoda, east of Phnom Penh.
We prepared boiled chicken to offer the *neakta,*

to ask them for safe passage to my son's house.
We reached home, Chbar Ampeou,
in mid-February, '79.
Our house was empty—not one of my books remained—

យើញតែកំណាព្យ *Emily Dickinson*
មួយសន្លឹកគត់ ។
អស្ចារ្យមែន ស្មាំដៃ ប៉ុល ពត!
ប៉ុណ្ណឹងហើយនៅមាន រៀតណាម លេបគ្របាក់ កម្ពុជា ទៀត ។

នៅនឹងផ្ញាំងបន្ទប់ដេកខ្ញុំ
កំណាព្យសរសេរថា៖
"កុំជីអ៊ីរ៉ាន់ ប្រយ័ត្នគ្រោះថ្នាក់
ព្រោះតែលោកករិ បានតែខ្ញុំបានធំ ។"

just a single ragged page of Emily Dickinson.
It was terrible!—the manifestation of Pol Pot's vision.
Then on top of *these* horrors,
Vietnam would try to gulp down our country.

On the wall of my bedroom
someone had chalked this poem:
"Don't ransack this place—Danger! Beware!
Because of this poet, I'm a bigshot now!"

អាសូរដើមក្រសាំងទៅវត្តព្រែកពោធិ

កាលចិត្តប្រាំ ក្រសាំងទៅខ្សែរខ្លី
មនុស្សមូលមីរ ចោមសុីផ្លែក្រសាំង ។
ដល់ចិត្តប្រាំបួន ក្រសាំងក្រៀម
ដើមប្រឡាក់ឈាម មានសក់ជាប់ ។

កាលចិត្តប្រាំ មនុស្សចូលជ្រក
ពេលនេះខ្ញុំមក ឆ្លងពាសក្រសាំងងាប់ ។
ក្រសាំង – សោគក៏អភ័ព្ទ
ទមិឡ្យបោកសម្លាប់ កុមារគរជី ។

អាណោាចខ្លោចចិត្តអាណិតក្រសាំង
ឧក្សាតប្រធាំង ក្រសាំងអត់ស្ពី
ឧក្សាតវាថា កុមារចង្រៃ
ទុកធ្លូន់ផែនជី ប្រល័យល្លជាង ។

វាថា "ដកស្មៅ ដកឲ្យអស់បួស
ទុកនាំទឹស ដុះលើសដើម" កម្មឫស្មៅសាង
ក្រោយរៀតណាមលុកស្រុកបាន
ខ្ញុំវិលផ្ទាន ស្មាក់វត្តព្រែកពោធិ ។

ខ្យ្លាយខ្វាំង កម្ម៉ាងអស់ ដោយជម្ងឺ
ខ្ញុំដកលើកុជិ – ផុំក្ខិនឈាម
ដកពុលក់ទេ – ដល់ព្រាហាម
ចុះភ្នាមក្រោមកុជិ – អង្គាមលុបឈាមកម្រាស់មួយម៉ែត្រ ។

THE KRASANG TREE AT PREK PO
for Joe Pohl

In '75 the krasang tree was green,
bore fruit for the soup of all the villagers.
By '79, the krasang tree had withered, its thorns
adorned with the hair of babies, its bark bloodstained.

In '75 the krasang tree was surrounded
by people seeking refuge.
By '79, the krasang tree was surrounded
by babies' skeletons, smashed

against its trunk by Utapats.
The Utapats said: "To annihilate
grasses, uproot them daily!" O, Grass!
What sin has the grass committed?

After the Vietnamese invasion
I followed the Mekong home.
I stopped to rest here, exhausted, sick.
On the second floor of the abandoned ashram

I stretched out to sleep in pitch darkness,
but the smashed skulls out there made me tremble.
Half asleep, I heard the moaning souls
of children beg for explanation:

ពិតជាទេីបប្រហារមនុស្សចោលថ្មៗ ។

យប់នោះខ្ញុំពួលប្រលឹងកុមារថ្ងូរ៖
"ម៉ែ! ម៉ែ! ម៉ែ!
"ម៉ែអើយ អើយម៉ែ កូនឧសអ្វី?
បានផាទមិឡ្យវៃប្រល័យកូន -
ចាប់ជេីងកូនបោកនឹងដេីមក្រសាំង ។
កូនទេីបកេីតមកចំស្រុកច្បាំង
កូនពុំដែលទាំងស្គាល់មុខម៉ែផង

ម៉ែ! ម៉ែ! ម៉ែ! កូនឧសអ្វី?

តេីសត្ខុឧត្បាតចង់បានអ្វី
បានផារាវ៉ៃកូនព្រះចោល
ផតក្រែងវៃអងព្រះឡ្យៃឥន ។
ម៉ែ! ម៉ែ! ម៉ែ! កូនឧសអ្វី?"

វិញ្ញាណកូន្ឋក្រសាំងឈ្លក់ឈាមក៍ថ្ងូរវៃរ
សត្ខុឧត្បាតប្រល័យទាំងផ្ទៃ ទាំងផ្ញា
សាច់ឈាមជនជាតិឯង រួមទាំងវុក្ខា
ទាំងអស់ គ្មានពេលគេចរួច!

"Ma! *Oeuy! Oeuy!* Ma! Ma!　　／　　What had we done wrong?
The Utapats slaughtered us　　／　　grasping our feet to
smash us with no mercy　　／　　breaking our skulls
　　　　　　against the krasang tree.

Our misfortune to be born　　／　　in the middle of a war—
never to learn our mothers' faces;　／　　what did the Utapats want of us?
Why were the Utapats　　／　　against God's children?
　　　　　　How dare the Utapats belittle God!"

That night, the smell of blood stayed with me.
At dawn, I went downstairs to find
rice husks spread over blood a meter deep:
evidence of a massacre more recent.

Then I heard the choked soul of the krasang tree,
drowned in the blood of infants. The Utapats
had killed its fruit with the fruit of our loins.
Neither had a chance to escape.

Part 4

❧ ❧

The Wilderness of Trakuon

JANUARY 1979 – 1991

ត្រឡប់រកពុក

ពេលកូនចេញទៅ ពុកនៅលើគ្រែ
ញាក់ញ័រគ្មានល្ហែ ពុកនៅងងោ
អត់បាយ អត់ទឹក ពុកពឹងពុទ្ធោ
ក្នុងប្រាណពេញពោរដោយក្តីឈឺផ្សា ។

ពុកពុំទៅទេ នៅភារនាធម៌
ប៉ុល - ពត បង្ខាំង បុត្រពីបិតា
ពេលនេះកូនមក ពុកបង់សង្ខារ
តើពុកអវនា ខ្លាចផ្សា – យ៉ាង – ណាទៅ!

កាលឆ្នាំចិតប្រាំទីនេះ អាស្រម
យាយតាប្រឹងខំអង្គុយរកផ្ទេរ
ដោយចិត្តឡេីយណាយ លែងចង់កើតនៅ
អន្ធង់ទុក្ខជ្រៅ ចង់ទៅនិព្វាន ។

ឥឡូវ ទីនេះ សុទ្ធ ប្រែនាម
យេីញស្មើស្រក់ឈាម ឡប់អស់វិញ្ញាណ
ព្រោះចង់ផ្សេសទុក្ខ ខ្ញុំខំប្រឹងរៀន
ផុត ម៉ា ជួប ម្យ៉ន សុទ្ធ ទុក្ខសោកសៅ ។

"ព្រា ត្រស់ អញ្ចាញ – អេីយ ដេីមរាំង
ពីប្រាំង ចិតប្រាំ ទីនេះ ឱ
នៅរស់ យកធម៌ ជាលំនៅ
ឥឡូវ ធាតុឱ នៅរណ្តៅ៎ណា?"

SEARCHING FOR DAD

for Lorraine Ciancio

When I left, Dad sat on his bed,
wanting to go through his shakes in private.
With no food or water, Dad lived on Buddha
while his body became covered with sores.

He refused to leave. He wanted to meditate.
Pol Pot separated me from my Teacher.
When I return, I find him gone.
Dad, what miseries did you suffer?

In '75, it was ashrams everywhere.
Old men and women who were fed up
with reincarnating into this life of pitfalls,
sought ways to reach Nirvana.

Now, in '79, I see only aquatic bushes.
I break into a cold sweat. I get dizzy;
no matter what the ideology du jour,
there is always the same lament.

Oh, trees in whose roots the fish spawn,
in the dry season of '75, my dad was still here.
He was alive under the sanctuary of worship.
Now, in what grave does his skeleton lie?

លោកជាមេជាងសាងសីលទាន
វិហារ វិមាន រាំង ប្រាង្គ ប្រា
ក៏ ត្រូវ ប៉ុល-ពត ផ្តាច់ជីវ៉ា
កំទេច បញ្ញា ញាណា គ្មាន ស្វាយ ។

ស្នេហ៍អើយ អើយស្នេហ៍ ចៅល្ងនគ្គ
ចៅស្ងរ ស្នេហ៍ផ្លើយ ចៅឆ្អានកាយ
ឲ្យតែស្នេហ៍ប្រាប់ ចៅស្ងមថ្វាយ
កេសាងផ្នាយ ព្រះសិអារ្យ ។

ឱស្នេហ៍ជើងក្រាស់ ស្នេហ៍កធ្លើយ
ចិញ្ចៀនស្នេហ៍ ផ្លើយ សូមវាចា
អដ្ឋធាតុ ឆី អញ នៅត្រង់ណា
មេត្តាប្រាប់អញ ឲ្យបាត់ខ្វល់ ។

❧ ❧

"ជើងមេយដូចជើងមុង ជើងទុងដូចជើងទា"
ប្រជាវេទនាដោយសារស្តេច
បាត់បង់ជីទឹកដោយជំទារស្នេហ៍ពេជ្រ
ប្រែ បាត់ វាលលេច ដោយអវិជ្ជា

ពុទ្ធោ កម្មអី តែកម្ពុជា!

                                    —មីនា ១៩៧៩

He was a builder, followed the precepts, gave alms.
He built temples, châteaux, palaces, stupas.
Yet Pol Pot killed him.
Annihilated his genius without regret.

O grasses, your grandson begs you—
if the grandfather grasses know
the whereabouts of my father's grave,
I shall shave my head in thanks.

O grass of thickets, grass
of sticking burrs, where is
the skeleton concealed?
Tell—and I shall ask no more of you.

❇ ❇

The horizon is like the hem of a mosquito net, pelican feet
like duck feet. We've been living in misery
because of our king, eclipsed because ladies adore diamonds,
our forest turned to deserts out of ignorance.

Oh, God! Why Cambodia?

—March, 1979

សក្តិទេវរាជទស្សនាកម្ពុជា

កាលអង្គរទេវិន្ទ
រដ្ឋកម្ពុជា

ទ្រង់ស្ដេចមិមន្ត
ក្រោយរាជ្យ ប៉ុល ពត
ផុវិញ្ញស៊ីមា ។

ចរចុះមកទត
ស្ដេចចរចេញទត

ទតទាំងអង្គរ
ព្រះកែរមរកត

ប្រាសាទបរវ
ស្ដេចចន្ទុលថា
ល្ងចអស់ទៅហើយ ។

ទតព្រះវិហារ
មហាចោរមារ

នៅតែក្រទ្បើ
នេះកម្ពុកម្ពុជា

តែបុត្រកុំបិ
ទេណាបុត្រអើយ
ពិទ្រព្យនេះណា ។

ខកចិត្តាឡើយ
បុត្រកុំព្រួយឡើយ

បុត្រតាំងសូរ្យតិ
បុត្រចង់គង់ជន្ទ

បុត្រកាន់ខន្តី
ឈប់សេពសុរា
វីករវើលរល់ ។

ចាំលើកសាសនា
ស្ដួយដល់បិតា

បិតាប្រាថ្នា
ពិច្ឆរាំងកាប់ចាក់

បង្ក្លាក់អសុរា
ពញ្ញាក់ឲ្យយល់
ព្រះពុទ្ធដីកា ។

ឲ្យរាលប់ខួល
ឲ្យវានឹកដល់

តែទាស់ចោបិ
ម្លេចឲ្យលេងពស់

ផូបគ្រោះទុក្ខភ័យ
ពិសកាចអស្ចារ្យ
មនុស្សមើលពុំកើត ។

ស្ដេកស្ងាំងកាយា
ជ្រាបពេញកាយា

បីប្រញាប់វីល
ផ្សុំឱិសឋទិព្ធ

ទោថានមើល
ព្យាបាលកុមារ
ថាបិចោលបុត្រ ។

ចាត់ពេឲ្យទេព្ទា
បុត្រកុំសង្ការ

ចាំពេលសាន្តត្រាណ
កត់ជាតម្រា

បិនិងវីលថ្ងាន
សារតាសុទ្ធ សុទ្ធ
តំណតកក្ល័ ។

ស្ងូត្ររៀងប្រាប់បុត្រ
ទុកជាទំនុក

—ខែ មិថុនា ១៩៨៤

VISITATION

for Galway McCullough

When Devinda showed up
in Cambodia, after Pol Pot's regime,
he went to observe the borders;
his motive: to end internal strife.

His real reason: the constant cries
of all the sentient beasts throughout the land
were keeping them up nights
in the Heavenly Realm.

He visited the ruins at Angkor,
he visited the Emerald Temple in the palace,
and then he came to my house to counsel me
not to worry about what the enemy had taken:

"My son ought to persevere—
a person endowed with forbearance
is always loved by gods and men.
By so doing, my son shall restore religion.

You would be wise not to indulge in alcohol—
its odor is offensive to those in your Heavenly Father's realm . . .
it will contribute to the rise of chaos,
and sentient beings in this land will suffer perpetually.

Your Father wishes to end this war, but I'm distracted—
my grandchild is too sick;
What in the world! My son let him play with a snake!
Now its venom permeates his liver, his marrow.

Your Father has to return to the Heavenly Realm
to order Dhornvatrei to prepare medicines.
Don't think that your Father has abandoned his son—
it will take a year to dry those preparations.

When peace prevails over this land
Your Father will come to elucidate our history
so that his son can record it once and for all.
Now your Father bids his son good-bye!"

—June, 1984

ឆាកកំប្លែងនៅមីទ្ទីងពង្រឹងភូមិឃុំ

"សូមគោរព ដូន-តា
មា មីង បងស្រី បងប្រុស
ចំពោះក្មួយប្រុស – ស្រី
ជាទីរាប់អាន ៖

កុំស្រែកដូចឆ្មា;
កុំថាដូចប្រេត;
កុំមាក់ងាយមនុស្ស;
កុំផ្ទុះដូចព្រាប ។

ក្រោមការដឹកនាំដ៏ឈ្លាសវៃ
នៃបក្សប្រជាជនបដិវត្តកម្ពុជា
សង្គមយើងមានប្រជាធិបតេយ្យមែន
យើងអាចស្ទួយទិតៀនតាមចិត្ត ។

លើកលែងតែស្រឡាញ់លទ្ធិប្រជាធិបតេយ្យ ។
បើហ៊ាន បក្សនិងការពារជននោះ
ប្រគល់បន្ទប់មួយអោយនៅ
ជាមួយសង្កើចនិងមុសមិនខាន ។

យើងឃើញហើយ
កុំថាតែវៀតណាម
រាប់តែសូវៀតក៏ត្រូវរ
មកបំរើយើងដែរ ។

HUMOR AT THE MEETING
TO STRENGTHEN PHUM KHUM

"Dear grandma, grandpa,
uncles, aunts,
my beloved sisters and brothers,
my esteemed nephews and nieces:

Don't meow like a cat,
don't chatter like devils,
don't belittle mankind, and don't
shit all over everything like pigeons.

Our society, under the clever leadership of the Cambodian People's Party,
is very democratic—we may autocriticize anytime we wish;
if anyone writes that he loves freedom and democracy,
the party will protect him in a safe cell.

You see, even the Soviets and Vietnamese
have come from far away to serve us,
to help us take the place of those killed by Pol Pot
by interbreeding with us, especially the Vietnamese.

Vietnamese troops help us eat *trakuon*—unwanted weeds.
They help us cut trees, catch fish,
hunt tigers, eat dogs,
and let us have free time to contemplate the sky.

រៀតណាមមកជំនួស :
អ្នករដ្ឋការ ទាហានសំឡេះ
សម័យ ប៉ុល-ពត ។ ជួយបង្កាត់ពូជ
បង្កើនប្រជាជនឱ្យដល់ ៨លាននាក់ ។

ទាំងរៀតណាមជួយស៊ីក្រក្កន – ស្មោចច្រៃ ;
ជួយកាប់ឈើព្រៃ – ជម្រកអ្នកគស្ស៊ី ;
នេសាទត្រី បាញ់ខ្លា ដំរី ស៊ីផ្ទេ ;
ទុកពេលទំនេរឱ្យយើងមើលមេឃកំសាន្ត ។

ឥឡូវកម្មជាសម្បូណិណាស់ ៖
មានផ្ទះដំរីប្រាបីរ៉ាវលុង;
មានផ្ទះមាន់ចូលរបោចស្គាប;
មានផ្ទះចាបហើរចូលរបោចអាម ។

បងប្អូនទាំងឡាយ ៖
នេះហើយភ័ព្វវាសនាយើង
រាតែអញ្ចឹង រាល់កាល
ឱ្យតែអ្នកដឹកនាំមានអ្នកបំរើជាបរទេស

តែស្គាមិនដុះផង ។ ធម្មតាទេ!
កុំព្រាយ – ដេកចាំតែកើតទុក្ខទៅ!"

—កញ្ញា ១៩៨៥

Cambodia now is very prosperous:
there are houses in which
seven elephants can dance the
waltz, tango, or fox-trot with ease;

There are also houses that,
when a cock gets in,
it doesn't even have room to turn around,
and houses so squat that even a bird can't fly through.

Dear compatriots,
it's what you get, it's the status quo—
whenever leaders are served by outsiders
it's only natural!—even grass can't grow."

—1985

របាំ ទេព កញ្ញា

កេសារំសាយ   អណ្ដេតសាយភាយ
ចាំងពណ៌សុវណ្ណ   សម្មស្សពណ៌ភ្នក
ចក្ខុភាងភាន់   អរាំពើនព័ន្ធ

              របាំអំបៅ ។

វាយោរំភើយ   ធម្មជាតិផ្ដល់ហើយ
បែគងរាលស្ងោ   ទ្របាទទេពកញ្ញា
ផតបិហ្មងសៅ   គយគន់យូរទៅ

           ជាប់នៅនេត្រា ។

ព្រះជាសាក្សី   គង់កេរនាគបី
របាំស្ងួគ៌ា   ស្ដេងថ្ងៃប្រាហស្បត៍
ឲ្យខ្ញុំទស្សនា   ទុកជាទ្រព្យា

           អង្គអញ្ញត្តទៅ ។

                              —យប់ ២២ មិថុនា ១៩៨៦ ០៣០០ ភ្លឺ

THE ANGEL PERFORMS
A HEAVENLY DANCE

for Ray and Stella Young Bear

An immaculate carpet of grass;
greenness stretches beyond the horizon.
An angel with hair the color of gold
and the complexion of polished ivory

sways her body with the grasses.
As she dances a classical ballet
her long hair floats in the air
in a pattern which dazzles my eyes.

Then she dances in the manner of a butterfly.
The breeze keeps raising her hair in an aureole.
The longer I contemplate her dance
the more indescribable its beauty becomes.

Only God is my witness to this.
Oh, Nagaraja's pearl,
It's unbelievable! I shall
treasure this scene in my mind forever!

—3:00 A.M., June 22, 1986

ប៉ុល ពត ថ្មី

ផុតពីក្រញ៉ាំខ្លា
ពើបនឹងក្រពើ ។
ផុតពីរបបប្រល័យពូជសាសន៍
ប៉ះអនុត្តរភាពនិយមពីទិសបូពិ៌ ។

ទឹកហួតបាត់ទៅក្នុងអាកាស
ហើយក្លាយជាភ្លៀង
ធ្លាក់ស្រោចលើដែនគោកផ្នក
រាប់ភ្លេច ។

ទួលខ្ពះក្លាយជារាលស្រែ
ស្ងៀលាស់ ផ្កា ផ្លែ សិបដងទៅហើយ
តែកុមារនៅស្វែកដណ្ដប់ផ្ទៃងទ្បេត
          – នៅតែបេះស្ទឹកឈើព្រៃ
          – នៅតែដកមើមស្ពៅ
សុំសំរន់ក្រពះដដែល ។

ខ្ញុះរកតែបាយកកមួយគ្រាប់ជាប់ផ្ទាំងក៏គ្មានផង ។
ជរាស្រែកថ្ងូរ យំសោកដោយបាត់
ចៅ កូន ឯ "កៃ" ។
អ្នកឈឺស្រែកទ្ទួញ បែរ ដុកទ័រ
សិតុយទារ សើចក្លាកក្លាយ ។

លំបាកវេទនាជូនទៅប្រជាជន ។
កសិផលជូនវង្សាភិបាលក្លេងក្លាយ ។
ជ័យជំនះជូនឧត្តមសេនិយសម្ល៉ាប់ជាតិឯង ។
ហើយអំណាចជូនទៅអាយ៉ងហាណូយ ។

NEO–POL POT

Free from tigers,
but facing crocodiles;
free from genocidal regimes,
I have to endure the usurpers from the east.

Water has evaporated into the sky,
turned into rains countless times
showering the whole land of Kok Thlok.
The mounds have become flattened into paddy fields.
Neem trees have bloomed, borne fruit more than ten years,
yet emaciated children still fetch
             —edible wild leaves
             —grass roots
appeasing their hunger.

Some don't even have bi-kok.
The old sob, grieve from losing
their grandsons, children at KO-5.
The sick groan, while doctors
lounge nearby laughing at them.

Hardships to the peasants,
crops to the fake government,
to the generals
victories based on killing those of their own race,
and power to the Hanoi puppets.

ខ្មែរបាន : មចូ ការណ៍ចាប់ អវទនា
ភាគសម្បត្តិផ្ទុនអ្នករត់គយ
(លោកជំទាវផំអាចម៌គោ) ឡើងមាន
ដោយភូរលើខ្លួងអ្នកស្មោះត្រង់
កំសាន្តកាយសប្បាយហ៊ុំហាបានទៅអ្នកបោកប្រាស

បារមីទាំងឡ្បាយត្រូវភាន់ភាំង
ដោយបណ្ឌិតបិទមាត់
ខ្លាចការផ្ដាល់គប
មន្ត្រីស្មោះត្រង់ដកខ្លួនថយសំងំស្ងៀម

ខ្មែររងគ្រោះទៅជាប្រមឹក
ដឹកទឹកភ្នែកផ្លូវស្រវឹងរាល់រដូវ
បំបាត់ទុក្ខព្រួយនិងការតូចចិត្ត
តែធាតុរសាប់រសល់នៅតែមានដដែល

ឱ នគរគោកផ្លូកអើយ
មាតុភូមិជាទីស្នេហារបស់ខ្ញុំ
តើត្រូវអស់ទឹកភ្នែកផ្លូវប៉ុន្មានរដូវទ្បៀត
អស់ស្រា ស ប៉ុន្មានលីត្រទ្បៀត
ទើបយើងបានលើកកែវជល់គ្នា
ដើម្បី "សេរីភាព និង លទ្ធិប្រជាធិបតេយ្យ ?"

—១៩៧៩ – ១៩៩១—

To the Khmers: death, lamentations, and suffering.
Wealth to the smugglers,
wives of big shots who ride to riches
on the backs of hardworking Cambodians;
a life of leisure to prevaricators.

Local deities are bemused
by wise men who keep silent
from fear of reprisals.
Faithful ministers "retire" from public service.

Kampalm and rice wine inebriate
Khmer victims from season to season,
drowning sorrows and resentments,
yet restlessness still prevails.

O, Nokor Kok Thlok,
my beloved!
How many more liters
until we propose the toast
for freedom and democracy!

—1979 – 1991

ទ្រាំរស់ព្រោះជាតិ

កែវប្រាក់មាសពេជ្រ   អាគារវាប់ភ្លេច
ពុំបានគិតគូរ   ថាជ័យភ័ណ្ឌ
ទាំងគ្រែតុទ្   សម្បត្តិសម្បូរ
ចាសម្បត្តិរដ្ឋ ។

គិតអីគ្រូងង   សព្ទផ្ទះសម្បេង
ម៉ូតូយន្តរថ   គិតជាតិល្អជាង
ទ្រទ្រង់ពាក្យសក្យ   សុខចិត្តកំសត់
ព្រោះស្រឡាញ់ផ្ទនជាតិ ។

ញញឹមសង្ឃឹម   ព្រាលប់ព្រាល៊ិម
ខិតខំឧិឃ្យាត   ថែទាំរោងចក្រ
ភ្លេចក្តីនឿយហត់   សង្ឃឹមថាជាតិ
ឆានឡើងរុងរឿង ។

ប្រហុកអំបិល   ម្ទូរស្ល៊ឹកអំព៊ិល
បាយពោតនៅសៀង   បំរើប្រជា
បែបបទឃ្លៀងមៀង   សង្ឃឹមថុំថ្មើង
មិនយូរគីធាប់ ។

សក់ស្ដើងស្បែកក្រាស់   កាលហ្ួសរហ័ស
បាត់ទៅគ្មានស្ួរ   ស្ងាយលាស់ច្រិនដង
ទូលខ្នះជាអ្ួរ   ធ្ើការយូរៗ
មានចេញក្រចូល ។

I TRY TO SURVIVE FOR MY NATION

Silver, gold, rubies, sapphires, diamonds,
apartments and villas innumerable,
but I'm not interested; I regard them as booty.
Tables, beds, radios, TVs, cameras . . . the list goes on—
Aren't they the common property of the state?

My family is small—
why should I bother with those things?
Why should I be a slave to material?
I'd rather be destitute than abandon my vows.

Bursting with hope
I have worked from dawn to dusk
restoring factories, gathering machinery, spare parts,
warehousing them for safekeeping.

Even though there is not much to eat
still I am proud like Grandpa Kleang Moeung
hoping the country will soon be happy and prosperous.

My hairline recedes, my skin thickens,
time slips by without fanfare.
After thirteen years of service to my country
my savings are gone; my pension, poverty.

ចិញ្ចឹមជីវិត   ខ្លាចធម៌ទុច្ចរិត
ខ្លាសបាបជាមូល   គ្មានអិស្សកប៉ាន់
លោកអ្នកកំពូល   បានទុគ្គិតចូល
                    លុកដែនអាត្មា ។

ឈឺដុះមាត់ច្រាំង   បើមាត់ត្រពាំង
សំណាងរាសនា   តែច្រាំងទន្លេ
នៅកម្ពុជា   រាល់ខែវស្សា
                    បាត់អត់សណ្ឋាប់ ។

ចិត្តមេស្រុកដែក   ផតបិរាវែក
ទោះរស់ទោះងាប់   ចិត្តបានឆ្កេផ្ធា
ការពារដែនភព   ការពារធនទ្រព្យ
                    បំផេវ័គ្គន័បិ ។

ទោះសត្តូឆ្មាត   មាក់ងាយប្រមាថ
ផ្ធិបាបជាន់ឈ្លី   ជេរភ្លេគិះដេ្យល
បញ្ចូនទៅព្រៃ   ខ្ញុំកាន់ខ្លួន្តី
                    ទ្រាំរស់ព្រោះជាតិ ។

I'm afraid of evil deeds
and I'm ashamed of sin.
I have no bribes to offer my superiors—
that's why poverty prevails over me.

The trees growing on the banks of lakes
are lucky, but if they grow
on the Mekong in Cambodia,
they are washed away every monsoon season.

The heart of Grandpa Dek
never shrinks from responsibilities
alive or dead—I have taken vows:
serving people and the Triple Gem.

Even though these ghouls look down
on me, trample my intellect,
insult me and send me to the fronts,
I try to survive for my nation.

សច្ចៈប៉ៈសាច់ក្មេ

មាន់រងារស្រេក   មេយអាទិត្យហោក
បំភ្លីអាស៊ូ   សូរ្យសែងត្រចៈ
យើញច្បាស់ប្រុសស្រី   ម្ងឺម្ងៗធ្វើការ
ញ្ញាប់ជើងញ្ញាប់ដៃ ។

អាយតនៈក្រៅ   ច្បាស់ថែសក្រឡេៗ
តែទាស់ហាច្ចទ័យ   មិនយល់ទេសោៈ
ចក្ខុវិស័យ   ម្ងួយថ្ងៃម្ងួយថ្ងៃ
ទល់មេយចិទវិញ ។

សេដ្ឋកិច្ចល្អតលាស់   គ្មានអ្នកជំទាស់
លាស់ខ្លួអ្នកទិញ   លាស់ភ្ងាមចាស់ភ្ងាម
រល្លួយទេវិញ   ព្រោៈអីទំនិញ
ទំនិញផុៈ ។

សញ្ញាតិកម្ពុជា   មិនបាច់រៀបការ
ព្រឹកឡ្ងៀងយើញផុស   នៅៗច្បារអំពៅ
កើតភ្ងាមសក់ស្ងុៈ   ធ្លេញបាក់ធ្លេញជ្រុៈ
កើតភ្ងាមចាស់ភ្ងាម ។

ត្រងំណាស់សេ្ងាៈណាស់   លក់ថ្មីទិញចាស់
ពន្ធត់សង្គ្រាម   មេីល់ខ្ងុំមេីលមេីល
លើកភ្ងាមជាក់ភ្ងាម   មិនបាច់ទិមទាម
រកស៊ីលល្ងាច ។

THE ENTRÉE CONFRONTS THE WORD KEEPER
for Rowena Torrevillas

Roosters crow   the sun tears the sky
clearing Asia.   It's blindingly bright.
We can see men and women   walking briskly
            to work.

Their physical senses   experience their circumstances clearly
but their minds   do not grasp what's really happening;
I see clearly, though,   from one day to the next
            till the sky closes its door.

They say the economy develops—   no one dare criticize.
A lot of goods, but no buyers,   imported, but secondhand;
they rot and rust,   for these goods
            are used goods.

Quasi-Cambodians   don't even have to be born here—
every morning they crowd   at Chbar Ampeou;
they are born with gray hair   broken teeth—
            just born, they are old right away.

Very honest, very loyal, our leaders trade our resources for worn-out junk
to quell the war   "Look at me now!
Ideal business   without a hitch;
            I can return by sunset.

ចេះតែអញ្ចឹង   បើច្បាស់ចង់ដឹង
ខ្ញុំមិនបន្ទាច   ខ្ញុំឃើញនឹងភ្នែក
អស់លោកអ្នកខ្លាច   ពេលត្រង់ពេលល្ងាច
                    មួបទិញឡើងគុ ។

អាទិ-អាហិន   សុទ្ធដង្ហាយចិន
សាច់ភ្លេមគ្រប់មុខ   បានផ្ទោះរបង
ចូលសំងំសុខ   អ្វីៗគ្រប់មុខ
                    សុំសុខពីលោក ។

Why should you hesitate?   If you want to know how . . .
I'm not scaring you, am I?   I've seen with my own eyes
those high authorities   at noon and evening—
      the magic food sits on their table,

Hennessy Whiskey—   all are Chinese gifts.
Entrées of all kinds   jump over the fence
get into the house   anything imaginable
      in exchange for their signatures."

Hou Leng, my subordinate, explains to me how the she-Minister of Industry gets rich overnight. He tells me that if I'm not corrupt like the communists, I won't be able to continue working with them.

"Enter the river at the bend,
enter the capital through the country."

ឆាកកំប្លែងផ្គត

ឆ្ងាំកោម្មយ ឆ្ងាំអស់សង្ឃឹម
ព្រាលប់ព្រាលឹម នាំគ្នាផឹកស្រា
អ្នកធាក់រុំម៉ក និង ខ្ញុំផ្ទួបគ្នា
នៅផ្ទះអាចារ្យ ឡៀមលក់ស្រា ស ។

មួយគយ ពិរគយញញ៉ឹមដាក់គ្នា
ក្នុងចិត្តវេទនា មានក្លាយជាត្រ
អ្នកខ្លាបានដៃ អ្នកចេះភ្ញៀក ស
បាត់មុខរបរ ផឹកស្រាបៅ៉ថៃ្ង ។

ស្រវឹងស្រៀៀងៗ មិនហ៊ានស្រែកទេ
ដល់ពេលថ្ងៃជ្រេ ស្រែកច្រៀងប្រាប់ខ្មែរ –
"អាមេរិកនឹងវិល នឹងវិល – នឹងវិលមកកម្ពុជា
យួនវារលូនចេញដូចស្រមោចធុំក្លិនប្រេងកាត ។"

អតីតកាលឯងឆ្ងឹតមុខផុតមិនខាន
ខ្មែរយើងគ្រប់ប្រាណមុខបានផុតឃ្លាត
ទុក្ខទោសហើយឈ្នាយរក្រង់កែវសុទ្ធស្អាត
ឆ្នាំតិ្តប្រមាថ តារាវុងវៀង ។

ខ្ញុំសុំបរណាដល់លោកទាំងបី
ហ៊ុជមិញ ឡៀទិន តាមាក្សមេភ្លើង
គោងដឹងចុះថា មុនក្រុមខ្ចៅៗឡៀង
ពួកយើងគ្នានព្រាយពីមួបអាហារឡៀយ ។

MAD SCENE

In those days of despair, in 1991,
at dusk, at dawn, we drank rice wine.
Pedicab drivers and I would gather
at our mentor's shack, the rice wine merchant.

After one or two belts, we began to smile at each other,
but inside we bore agonies; we'd been rich but now were poor.
Illiterates were in power; the eyes of the educated were white with fear—
they'd lost their jobs and become drunkards.

While still sober, we didn't dare squawk.
But when afternoon came, I sang for the Khmers—
"Americans shall return, return to Cambodia!
And Yuon shall vanish, vanish like red ants at the smell of petroleum,
like red ants at the smell of petroleum."

And "out from the gloomy past"
all Khmers shall be removed from
misery, disdain, and at last we will
stand "where the white gem of our bright star will cast."

I declare that, yes, I'm afraid of you Three:
O, Ho Chi Minh! O, Len-in! O, Grandpa Marx!
You should know that before the illiterate came to power
we never worried about food.

គាំងពីអស់លោករំដោះវណ្ណៈ
រកតែត្រកូនស្ម ក៏ពុំបានជង
អូ បាទ យើងមិនបាច់សុិទេ
ព្រោះអីលោកថា "អត់ធើ អត់សុិ"

ធ្វើអ្វីកើត
បើលោកជាន់ឈ្លី សិទ្ធិមនុស្ស
ទុកខ្មែរជាអាណានិកជនបែបថ្មី
ឯជីក៏ជាចំការមីនរបស់លោក អស់ទៅហើយជង ។

ពេលនេះខ្ញុំថ្លាយបង្គំទាំងបូនទិស
ហើយខ្ញុំសុំស្បថយ៉ាងឧឡារិកថា :
"ខ្ញុំសូមខ្លាចអស់លោកទាំងបីហើយ!
ហើយខ្ញុំឈប់ទឹកលោកទល់ភ្លើងធះកល្ប!"

ដំបូងសូរគឺល – រំពងទ្បេមស្រា
រួចសម្តក់គ្នា រំកីលគូថជយម្នាក់ម្ដង
ខ្ញុំនៅតែច្រៀង ដោយមានបំណង
ចិត្តបានបន់ផ្សង ឆ្ពោះ សេរីភាព ។

Since you came to liberate us,
there is not even aquatic grass to eat.
Oh, yes, we don't worry about eating
for you say, "no work, no eat."

How can we work
for you trample our human rights,
look down on Khmers as the neo-minority
while the land becomes your minefield.

Now I bow in the four directions,
and I solemnly pronounce:
"I'm really afraid of you THREE!
And I swear I will never dream of you forever, ever!"

First, cackles would burst out everywhere,
then the audience would wink at each other, furtively,
and retreat into the night, one by one.
Yet I crooned on, on the road to freedom.

សូម "អធិដ្ឋានពិសិដ្ឋ" ប្រែជាការពិត

"ជយោ សេរីភាព! ជយោ លទ្ធិប្រជាធិតេយ្យ!
ឋរាជ័យ ឋរាជ័យ អាអំពើជិះជាន់កំណាច!"
យើងស្រែកច្រៀងព្រមៗគ្នា
ឯសេចក្តីឈឺចាប់ក៏កើនឡើងរាល់ថ្ងៃដែរ ។

ខ្មែរ ស្អប់ ខ្មែរ
ខ្មែរចោទ គ្នាទៅវិញទៅមក សម្លាប់គ្នា
ផួនគូស្នេហ៍ កូនចៅ ទៅឲ្យក្រពើ
ក៏ព្រោះ លោភៈ មោហៈ ទាំឲ្យភ្លេចវិញ្ញាណ ។

148

ខ្មែរប្រុសស្រីសរសើរ ម៉ាក្ស – លេនីន
ជំនួសឱពុកម្ដាយ ឬ ព្រះពុទ្ធរបស់ខ្លួន
គេឲ្យប្រជាជនស៊ីត្រកួន
ផ្គាប់ម្ចាស់គេឲ្យសប្បាយចិត្ត ។

ទោះអណ្ដើកក៏លែងពង
អ្នកច្រឡើសបើស អ្នកទុច្ចរិត អាអត្ពូជ
ឆក់ទ្រព្យយកធ្វើមានទាំងយប់
ធ្វើយាតម្ដាយ កំទេចព្រះពុទ្ធ ។

ស្រែកខ្ញុំឡើងជ្រុញ
សក់ខ្ញុំក៏សូវ ផ្ងៃះពាក់កណ្ដាល
ក៏ព្រោះតែខ្លាចក្រពើពេលធ្វើ
ដំណើរកាត់វាលត្រក្ខន ។

MAY MY SACRED VOWS COME TRUE!

"Bravo, Liberty! Bravo, Democracy!
Down, down, the tyranny of a despot!"
We sing this in unison
while agonies multiply with each sunrise.

Cambodians hate their fellow Cambodians,
accuse each other, kill each other,
offer their lovers, their children to crocodiles,
for greed and foolishness daze their minds.

Men, women,
praise Marxism-Leninism,
instead of their parents or Buddha,
they let their people live on trakuon to please their lords.

Thus, turtles can't lay eggs anymore.
Scum, thieves, bastards
grasping at overnight fortunes
kill their mothers, destroy their Buddhas.

My skin is wrinkled,
my hair grizzled, half fallen out
from fear of crocodiles while journeying
across the Wilderness of Trakuon.

និងធ្វើឡ្បាកគេទុកចិត្ត
ខ្ញុំ ជំរុញ សម្ព័ន្ធខ្មែរដើម្បីសេរីភាព
ឲ្យស្រែកច្រៀង
ច្រៀងព្រមៗគ្នា –

នាំគ្នាបំពងសម្លេងឡើងហើយច្រៀង
ទាល់ប្រថពិនិងមេឃរញ្ជួយ
លាន់សូរឡើង ឯកនឹ "សេរីភាព"
បណ្ដោយឲ្យយើង
រីករាយឡើងខ្លស់ទាល់ទេព្តាស្វាប់ញ,
ទុកឲ្យរាងរ លាន់ដូចសមុទ្របោកច្រាំង ។
ច្រៀងចំរៀងពោរពេារដោយជំនឿ ដែលអតីតកាលងងឹតបានបង្រ្សៀនយើង,
ច្រៀងចំរៀងពោរពេារដោយក្ដីសង្ឃឹមដែលបច្ចុប្បន្ននាំមកឲ្យយើង,
យើងគោងឈមមុខនឹងសុរិយានៃថ្ងៃថ្មី,
គោះកូន គោះកូន យើង
ឆ្ពោះទៅមុខទាល់ជ័យជំនះបានមកយើង ។

ច្រៀង គោះយើងច្រៀង!
យើងនាំគ្នារីករាយ
ឡើងខ្លស់ទាល់ទេព្តាស្វាប់ញ,
ហើយឲ្យខ្លរ លាន់ញដូចសមុទ្របោកច្រាំង –
ហាក់ដូចយើងនៅស្រុកអាមេរិក!

លោកអើយ!
យើងនៅក្នុងវាលត្រក្ខូនសោះ
សុទ្ធតែក្រពើអត់ឃ្លាន ។
តទៅយើងស្រែករក "ពុទ្ធំ ធម្មំ ជាជម្រក
សង្ឃំ ជាគុណធម៌ការពារយើង – "
ខ្ញុំស្ងូគ្រយ៉ាងនេះ ប្រាំពីរដង វាល់ម៉ោង ។

—សម័យរវៀត-ណាម ត្រគតគ្រា ១៩៧៩ – ១៩៩០

To get on their good side,
I exhort the Khmer League of Freedom
to raise their voices in song,
to sing in unison—

> *Lift ev'ry voice and sing,*
> *Till earth and heaven ring,*
> *Ring with the harmonies of Liberty;*
> *Let our rejoicing rise*
> *High as the list'ning skies,*
> *Let it resound loud as the rolling sea.*
> *Sing a song full of the faith that the dark past has taught us,*
> *Sing a song full of the hope that the present has brought us;*
> *Facing the rising sun of our new day begun,*

Let us, sons, let us, sons,
> *March on till victory is won.*

Sing! Let's sing!
> *Let our rejoicing rise*
> *High as the list'ning skies,*
> *Let it resound loud as the rolling sea . . .*

As if we were in America!

Alas!
We're in the Wilderness of Trakuon
which is full of hungry crocodiles,
hence: "Buddham, Dhammam, be our refuge,
Sangham be our protector . . ."
I recite this seven times every hour.

—under Vietnamese suppression, 1979 – 1990

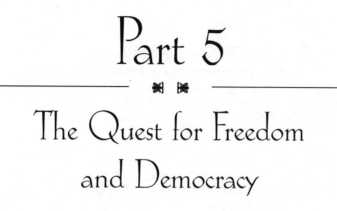

Part 5

The Quest for Freedom and Democracy

SEPTEMBER 1992 – 1998

ពេលដល់ ខ្យល់ល្អ ក្រ រសាយ

I.

"មនុស្សល្ងង់ណាមិនបានពិចារណាសេច្បានុភាពថៃរ
ហើយចូលទៅប្រយុទ្ធដោយរួសរាន់ មនុស្សល្ងង់នោះនឹងបានឱបមុខជារវជាប្រាកដ
នេះជាសច្ចៈឥត សង្ស័យឡើយ"
         — ភិក្ខុ ប៉ាង ខាត់ ឆ្នាំ ១៩៥៤

ឆ្នាំ ច ចិត្តសិបត្រូវឆ្នាំព្រាត់ប្រាស
ស្តេចព្រាត់ពីរាស្ត្រនិរាសនគរ
គាំងរវៃរួតក្នុងកម្ពុជារីករវរ
ប្រជាជាប់គររគេព្រាត់រវៃខ្មែរ ។

លន់ នល់ អាងមន្ត ឃ្លូនអាងសង្គ្រាម
ខ្មែរបង្ករលាមដណ្ដើមយកជ័យ
ខាល – ថោះ ព្រោះកម្មក្បូររវៃខ្មែរចូលព្រៃ
ប្រជាក្បិណក្ប្រៃយដួចត្រូវផ្គាសា ។

អសុរទមិឡ្យបានអំណាចក្របាមគាំទ្រ
ពាសពេញនគររសុទ្ធទុក្ខវេទនា
អសុរកាយមានពិតក្នុងកម្ពុជា
មនុស្សស៊ិត្ថា ម៉េធិខ្លាចកូន ។

II. ទ័ពអាសៃយសាស្ត្រដេញអសុរទមិឡ្យ
បូនឆ្នាំទ្រាំណាស់តែរស់មិនដល់
ជីវិតវិលរល់ផ្ទួបភ្ជិមរណា
ចោលប្រពន្ធបុត្រទាំងទុក្ខខ្លោចផ្សា
អសុរទមិឡ្យប្រហារកណ្ដាលស្មសាន ។

A FRESHENING WIND IS RISING

I.

> "The stupid leader who does not assess the strength of his enemy's
> army and jumps into battle unprepared will impale himself on the
> bayonets of his enemy."
>   —Rev. Pang Khat, 1954

The Year of the Dog (1970) was a year of separation:
the King abandoned his subjects by fleeing the country;
the Free World made war against the VC, and Cambodia
was in the line of fire—everybody turned on Cambodia.

The SEATO countries ganged up with South Vietnam—
Ta Khmao put his faith in talismans
while Vietnam relied on military science.
FANK shed the blood of FUNK, hoping to cull some glory from it.

The Year of the Tiger (1975) and the Year of the Rabbit (1976):
citizens were butted out of Phnom Penh
into the woods, where they fell into punji pits,
blasphemies blown back in their faces like spit in the wind.

The atheists came to power because Beijing supported them.
Misery hung over the countryside like a dense fog;
human vipers lurked in every cranny of Cambodia;
people ate each other; parents were terrified of their own children.

II. THE ALIENS ROUT THE ATHEISTS
For four years we slaves tried to survive, but couldn't—
running from death, we met death face-to-face;
the atheists mowed us down at every turn,
leaving our wives and children in agony.

មមៃ យក្សយួនគុំគួនអនេក
ដៃថ្រែកកាត់ព្រៃកាត់ព្រៃករុញច្រាន
ពីកើតពីជើងទមិឡ្យរត់ប្រាសប្រាណ
កាត់ព្រៃស្សារលាក់ប្រាណាស្រុកខ្ញុំង ។

ច កុរ ខាល ថោះ រលស់ជាតិខ្មែរ
ម្ប្រាញ់ ដល់ មមៃ ខ្មែរជាស្បូរភ្លាំង
អ្នកគង់ជីវិតវាងកាយស្តមស្តាំង
បារាំងយើញខ្លាចលែងហ៊ានដាក់ទោស

III.
    ចុះទឹកក្រពើ ឡើងលើខ្លា ចូលព្រៃបន្លា
    ចូលផ្សារឧនគរបាល

ថារួចពីខ្លា អរណាស់ខ្មែរយើង
ថារួចពីភ្លើង សង្គ្រាមប្រទូស្ត
ប៉ែរមកក្រពើលេបលើក្នាមេឈ្មស
ខ្មែរប្រុសរលស់លើសពី មមៃ ។

"កុ៥" ខ្មែរចាំជាប់ជាក់មិនភ្លេច
ចាន់-ស៊ុ ឧះខ្លួចព្រោះតែ គវ៉ា
កាលណោះគេថាៈ
"បងហត់នឿយណាស់ព្រោះឧំធ្វើការ
ឥឡូវ អាន់ ណា ទៅសំរាកទៅ

ពេឡ្យទៅ ហាណ្ឌយ អាន់ ណា
សំរាន្តសំរាក មាន អែម បម្រើ ។"

The Year of the Goat:
the giant had held a long-term grudge—
from the north and the east, it dogged the atheists
running wild across the forests, hand-to-hand in the rivers

brawling in the mountains, all the way to the
homeland of their ancient enemy.
In the Years of the Dog, the Boar, the Tiger, and the Rabbit
the Khmer population was decimated.

From the Year of the Cobra to the Year of the Goat
the Khmer people became fertile compost for the grasses.
Those who had stayed alive were walking skeletons—
even the Frenchies quivered, no longer our superiors.

III.
> *If you went into the water, there were crocodiles;*
> *on the land, tigers stalked you; in the woods,*
> *thorns in every thicket; in the market, cops everywhere.*

We all had smiles on our faces
because the Tiger had been driven from our vicinity.
We thought we had come through the war of genocide—

while observing the crocodiles from the banks
we saw them gulp down coffins whole—
even more men victimized than in the Year of the Goat.

The Khmer people have never forgotten A5.
Chansi was cremated because of his backtalk.
Our keepers proved to be very clever—

They said to him: "You've been working too hard,
Dong Chi, we'll send you to the hospital in Hanoi
for R&R—lots of teenage girls there to serve you."

IV. ព្យែរ ឬ ឆោត

ខ្មែរអើយ អើយខ្មែរ
កើតពីពោះមែ៎ម្ដេចទុក្ខឥតល្ហែ
រងទុក្ខរងទោសរាល់យប់ថ្ងៃខែ
ព្រាងព្រឹកថ្ងៃជ្រេខ្មែរយំរហូត ។

ខ្មែរ ធំ ខ្មែរ មាន មានដួចគេដែរ
សូមអស់ពួជខ្មែរខាងពហូសូត
ជ្រោងជាតិស្រោចស្រង់ជាតិខ្មែរគ្រង់សូត
ច – ផុត ឱ្យផុតពីបានអរចិ ។

158

ផ្ដាយចុះមិនទុស្សបំណងសោះទេ
ផ្ដាយតំកើងខ្មែរ ប្រជាធិបតេយ្យ
ជ្រោងទៅ ជ្រោង ទៅ! ប្រាកដជោគជ័យ
ខ្មែរៃថ្ងៃខ្លស់មុខកើតមនុស្សទេវៃ ។

—ឆ្នាំ ១៩៨២

IV. RETRIBUTION AND DECEPTION

Cambodians, you, like any other humans, were born
from your mother's womb. What is it about you
that brings such suffering down on your heads—
at daybreak, at noon, in the afternoon, always lamenting?

There are intelligent Cambodians, rich Cambodians,
the same as in any other nation—
O, please, you learned ones, don't betray our
innocent Cambodian brothers and sisters.

Before the Year of the Dog, before the Year of the Rat,
help lift Cambodians out of this bestial existence.
Please support them—don't wind up feeling repentent,
don't settle for safe and sound regrets.

Please support them—together we are going to be victorious.
When Cambodians become an esteemed people
in the eyes of the world, we will inherit heaven on earth.

—1982

សម្រែកអង្គរអង្គរពាជខ្មែររួមមហាសាមគ្គីជាតិ

សូមអស់ ករី	ករីប្រុសស្រី	ស្តាប់អង្គរស្រែក
ស្រែកទទួញទ្រហោរ	ព្រោះប្រេះបាក់បែក	ខ្លាំងនាំគ្នាបែក
	ចែកកម្ពុជា ។	
ប្រាសាទបាយ័ន	ស្រែកគគ្រឹកលាន់	អាសូរប្រជា
រយឆ្នាំរួចហើយ	នៅរងវេទនា	រស់ក្នុងទុក្ខផ្សា
	ព្រាត់ប្រាសកូនចៅ ។	
ស្តាប់បន្ទាយស្រី	យំស្រែកបែកថ្មី	ស្រីពៅសោកសៅ
ព្រោះសត្ថុងក្បាត	ប្រមាថស្រីពៅ	សុន្ទពុជពង្សខ្លៅ
	ប្រដៅអ្នកប្រាជ្ញ ។	
យក្ខនីឡើងផំ	ព្រោះចេះភ្លែងយំ	យំសុំអំណាច
ពិយក្សូណាមកុក	ដល់ផំគោងកាច	តែបើជាខ្លាច
	ខ្លាចពួកកក្ខប ។	
ករី កម្ពុជា	ផ្ទួយខាបកាព្យា	បរិហារ របប
ពន្យល់សត្តលោក	របប បន្ថប	កណ្ដៀរ កណ្ដូប

ចុះដល់ស្រែណោ ហិនហោចស្រែហ្មឹង ។

ក្រមង៉ុយចេងជា	កំណាព្យឃ្លោងឃ្យា	ទុកជាជំណឹង
តំណពីនោះ	មុខគង់តែជឹង	កាយនិងព្រលឹង
	មុខផ្ទួបស្ប៊ុទ្រាំ ។	

THE RUINS OF ANGKOR CRY OUT
FOR NATIONAL CONCORD

O poets!   poets male and female,   listen to the ruins!
They are wailing   for they have been decimated   by enemies fighting to rip
    Cambodia apart.

The Temple of Bayon   cries aloud   having pity on the Khmer people—
hundreds of years have passed   yet they suffer still,   live in agony, broken homes.

Listen to Banteay Srei   crying for lost husbands—   she laments
because evil beasts   impugn her soul;   they are culprits yet they counsel sages.

Witches become top officials;   they know how to moan   moaning for power
from Namkoc ogres,   and once they're in power   they abuse the natives
and spend their time   licking the feet   of those who wear patched clothes.

O, Cambodian poets,   please cast poems   to subdue the power of the hoe.
Enlighten the world   about hoes and patched outfits—   they are crucibles in disguise.

In the old days   Kram Ngoy composed   a simple ode
of potent words   that in the future   our bodies and souls would bear tyrannies:

"ទករថ្មើងហ្មែក   សប្បាយតែភ្នែក   ក្នុងចិត្តរងកម្ម
កូនប្រុសបណ្ដាច់   កុំភ្លេចបណ្ដាំ   កប្បាស់សូត្រថ្ងាំ
                       ត្រីម៉ាំលែងថៅក ។"

ប្រាសាទអង្គរ   ស្រុកអង្គរ ករ   ស្រុកយ័ំសៅសោក
ដោយទទឹងឡ្បឧត្បាត   កោងកាចស្មោកត្រោក   គំនិតកើតរោគ
                       គោកចតុម្ខ ។

អង្គររស្រុកហោ   អង្គរកូនចៅ   រ្ួមសុខ រ្ួមទុក្ខ
រ្ួម មហាសាមគ្គី   វំដោះភូមិស្រុក   ឯករាជ្យពេញមុខ
                       បូរណភាពទឹកជី ។

This country appears to be extraordinarily prosperous—
a facade attractive to the eyes
but decaying on the inside.
My optimistic son,
please remember my words—
cotton, silk, tobacco, and preserved fish will never be cheap.

Angkor Wat   our most sublime monument   weeps and sobs
because the beasts with two faces   brash and dirty-minded   fill in the four
    branches of the Mekong with waste.

Angkor Wat cries out,   soliciting her descendants: "Unite completely
live together   in both peace and war   to liberate our country
from tyranny   restore independence   and the integrity of our borders." | 163

ពញ្ញកទេព្តា
រៈកាត់ភ្នែកនិងជាក់កែវភ្នែកថ្មី

កិន បាននាំខ្ញុំទៅ
ការិយ៉ាល័យទី១នៅម៉ោង៧:៤៥ព្រឹក
"លោក អ្វី?"
ខ្ញុំបង្ហាញងកសារពេទ្យ ទៅតិលានុបដ្ឋាយិកា ។

តិលានុបដ្ឋាយិកាស្ទុកុំព្យូទ័រ
តែមួយភ្នែកប៉ុណ្ណោះ
គាត់ឲ្យខ្ញុំទៅបន្ទប់ផ្សាស់សំល្យេកបំពាក់
មេពេទ្យទទួលស្វាគមន៍ខ្ញុំយ៉ាងកក់ក្ត ។

"សូមស្រោតខោ-អាវឲ្យអស់ – ទុកតែខោទ្រនាប់ហើយ!"
ខ្ញុំព្រឹខ្លាក – ស្ង្យេកឡ្យើងសម្បុរគឺភ្ញាក់ពេញ
"នេះអាវហ្គាន ហើយនេះទ្រនាប់ជើង –
ទំរតលើគ្រែឲ្យស្រួលចុះ ។"

"តើលោកមានញាំអាហារ ឬ ទឹកពេលកន្លងអជ្រាត្រឬទេ?"
"អត់ទេ"
"តើលោកបានជាក់ *Tobrex* នៅភ្នែកស្ដាំទេ?"
"បានជាក់"

"ភ្នែកណាមួយដែលត្រូវរៈ?"
តិលានុបដ្ឋយិកាសួរ
"ស្ដាំ!"
"ឆ្វេ" ។

ANGELS

PROCEEDINGS OF MY CATARACT OPERATION
AND TRANSPLANTATION OF A NEW LENS

Ken brought me
to Office #1 at 7:45 A.M.
"Mr. U?"
I presented my medical documents.

The nurse chats with the computer.
In a minute
she recommends that I go to the surgical dressing room.
A mother nurse welcomes me warmly.

"Take your clothes off, please—everything except your shorts!"
I was solid with goose bumps.
"Here's a gown, and here are some slippers—
lie down on the bed and make yourself comfortable."

Have you taken any food or drink after midnight?"
"No."
"Have you put Tobrex on your right eye?"
"Yes."

Which eye are you going to have operated on?"
an angel nurse asks.
"Right."
"Good."

Sister ម្នាក់ចូលមកបន់ស្រន់៖
"ឱ ព្រះជេស៊ីស គ្រិស្ត
យើងសូមប្រគល់ជំនៀៀចំពោះទ្រង់ –
សូមឱ្យ សាម បានទទួលជោគជ័យក្នុងការវៈកាត់នេះ!"

នៅគ្រប់ទិសាន *Greg, Marlene, Cyndi,*
The First Mennonite Church,
សហគមន៍អ្នកនិពន្ធអន្តរជាតិ
ហើយជាពិសេស *Maggie Hogan* បន់ស្រន់ឱ្យខ្ញុំជួបសុខ ។

ពេលម៉ោង ៩:៤៥ព្រឹក ការវៈកាត់ចាប់ផ្ដើម ។
ខ្ញុំពួសម្ងែងយ៉ាងពីរោះ
"សុខសប្បាយជាទេ លោក យូ?" អេជ្ជបណ្ឌិតទេព្ធាសួរ
"សុខណាស់ អរគុណ!" ខ្ញុំចេះតែថាទៅ

ខ្ញុំពួសួរទេព្ធាបញ្ចេញឈ្មោះ
ឧបករណ៍ វៈកាត់យ៉ាងផ្ដែមល្អែម
ខ្ញុំចង់ឱ្យពេលវៈកាត់បានវែង
តែសម្ងែង "រួចហើយ" បានច្រានខ្ញុំចេញពីពេទ្យទេព្ធាទៅ ។

ខ្ញុំត្រូវគេរុញទៅបន្ទប់រង់ចាំវិញ
គេបានលើកអាហារឱ្យខ្ញុំ
មួយម៉ោងក្រោយមក ម៉ារិ ម៉ាហ្គី
បានដឹកខ្ញុំទៅផ្ទះនាង ថែទាំល់សៈរប្ួស ។

ស្អាត ប្រិមប្រិយ រាក់ទាក់ គួរសម ពិរោះអឺម៉្លះៈទេ –
ពិតជាបានសួតិមែន
ភ្នែកខ្ញុំភ្លឺច្បាស់តែក្នុងមួយអាទិត្យ
ភ្លីជាងកាលខ្ញុំនៅជាកុមារទៅទៀត ។

—ថ្ងៃទី ២៣ ខែ វិច្ឆិកា ១៩៩២

A Sister comes and prays
"O, Lord Jesus Christ,
in You we believe . . .
May Sam come through this cataract operation successfully!"

Elsewhere, Greg, Marlene, Cyndi,
the First Mennonite Church,
the International Writers,
and especially Maggie Hogan, pray for my well-being.

Time: 9:45. The operation begins.
I hear harmonious sounds.
"How are you, Mr. You?" the angel doctor asks.
"Fine, thank you." I say, pretending it's all make-believe.

I hear her pronounce the names
of surgical instruments in a sweet voice.
I wish the operation would take even longer,
but the word *finished* separates me from the angel doctor.

I am pushed back to the waiting room.
They serve me a meal.
In one hour, Mary Maggie
takes me to her house to recuperate.

Pretty, charming, nice, kind, sonorous—
it's a real heavenly realm!
In a week my right eye sees
more clearly than when I was a boy.

—November 23, 1992

ពិនិត្យភ្នែកឆ្វេងលើកទី១ ក្រោយការវះកាត់

I.

ពេលណាត់ជួបបានមកដល់
ពេលខ្ញុំកំពុងអង្គុយគិតដល់
ទ្វីបទាំងពីរ ពេទ្យទេព្តា
បានផុសនៅមុខខ្ញុំហើយញញឹម ។

ខ្ញុំក្រោកឈរគោរព
តែទេព្តាបង្វិលទៅវិញអត់ស្តី
ខ្ញុំដើតតាមស្នេហ៍ទិព្វ
ចូលក្នុងបន្ទប់ពិនិត្យ ។

សម្លេងថាៈ "អង្គុយលើកៅអីខ្មៅនោះចុះ ។"
– បើសិនទេព្តាមិនបញ្ជាក់ ប្រហែលខ្ញុំ
ជ្រើសខុសទៅហើយ ។ តែជាឥរិយាបទទេព្តាទេ ។

ពេទ្យទេព្តាបកស្បែចេញពីភ្នែកឆ្វេងខ្ញុំ
ហើយជូតទឹកភ្នែកថើៗ
ពេលយើងសំណេះសំណាលគ្នា ។
ខ្ញុំមានសំណាងមែន!

"បង្អោនចង្កាទៅមុខ"
តើអង្គុណារឹងនឹងភាពទន់ភ្លន់នេះ?
"បើកភ្នែកឲ្យធំ – ហើយសម្លឹងចំទៅមុខ!"
ទោះបីនាងមិនថាក៏ខ្ញុំនៅតែឮ "សូម" ។

FIRST CHECKUP ON MY LEFT EYE
AFTER CATARACT OPERATION

I.
The appointed time has arrived.
While I'm sitting with my mind
two continents away, my angel doctor
appears before me, smiling.

I stand up to salute her
but she pivots away without a word.
In a hypnotic spell, I float after her
to her consultation room.

She says, "Sit down on that black chair."
—almost as if were she not precise, I might
choose the wrong one. But that's just her manner.

She pulls the pad off my left eye,
gently pats away the discharge
while we're exchanging conversation.
What a godsend I've received!

"Lean your chin forward."
Who could resist her gentleness.
"Open your eyes wide . . . and look straight ahead."
Though she didn't actually say it, I still heard her say, "Please."

"ភ្នែកឆ្លងគ្រាន់បើជាងភ្នែកស្ងាំ!
តើលោកអាចគ្រឡប់មកក្នុងពេលមួយខែបានទេ?"
ខ្ញុំនឹកថាគួរតែឆាប់ជាងនេះ តែខ្ញុំត្រូវ
ស្ងាប់បង្គាប់ពេទ្យ ហេតុនេះខ្ញុំថា "ប្រាកដមែនណា ។"

II.
ក្រោយពិនិត្យលើកទីពីរ
ពេទ្យទញ្ចាអនុញ្ញាតឲ្យខ្ញុំទៅ ដេ-មញ្ញ
ចូលរួមពិធីបុណ្យចូលឆ្នាំថ្មី
និងទៅសូត្រកំណាព្យនៅ *Coe College* ។

ថ្ងៃពុធទី ១២ ខែ ឧសភា ម៉ោង ៨ ព្រឹក –
ការពិនិត្យចុងក្រោយ – ហាក់ដូចជាឃរណាស់ ។
រយៈពេលនេះ ខ្ញុំសប្បាយគយគន់បុប្ផា
និងសត្វល្អិតក្របល់អងដ្ឋាយ៉ាងសុខចិត្តសុខកាយ ។

ភ្នែកខ្ញុំបានស្រាលហើយ – ខ្ញុំមើលឃើញកាន់តែឆ្ងាយ
ខៀវច្បាស់ជាខៀវ ក្រហមច្បាស់ជាក្រហម ។ ល ។
សូមអរគុណព្រះជាម្ចាស់! សូមសម្ដែងកតញ្ញុតាដ៏ជ្រាលជ្រៅ
ចំពោះ *Lyse S. Strnad,* ធម្មន្ត្រី ។

—ថ្ងៃសុក្រទី ១៩ ខែ មិនា ១៩៩៣

"Your left eye is better than the right one.
Could you come back in one month?"
I wish to come sooner, but I must
obey her orders, so I say "of course."

II.
After the second checkup
she gives me permission to go to Des Moines
for the Khmer New Year celebration,
and to Coe College to give a reading.

Wednesday, May 12th at 8:00 A.M.—
my final checkup—seems a long time to wait.
In the interim, I enjoy gazing at blossoms
and tiny insects sucking up pollen.

My eyes feel rested—I can see far into the distance
and green clear green, red clear red, and so on . . .
Thanks be to God! My deepest gratitude to
Dr. Lyse S. Strnad, DHORNVANTREI!

—Friday, March 19, 1993

៦ មេបញ្ជាការ មេបញ្ជាការខ្ញុំ ចូរជារតុសក្កិសិទ្ធិ របស់ខ្ញុំ

ថ្ងៃព្រហស្បតិ៍ ទី ២៩ មេសា ១៩៩៣ ធាតុអាកាសប្អូរ –
គឺជាព្រហាមប្រកបដោយកំដៅល្ម
នៅម៉ោង ១០:០០ ព្រឹក
ខ្ញុំធ្វើដំណើរតាមផ្លូវ ហ្វីលបៀត ។

ស្ត្រីម្នាក់អោនចំកិតគូច ដោះអារជោា
ហើយញាត់ចូលក្នុងស្បោងស្ដាយ
ដូចជាព្រហើន បើសំឡឹងគូចគាត់
ដូចនេះធ្វើជាមើលកំប្រុកវិញ ។

វិញ្ញាណខ្ញុំអណ្ដែតត្រូវសេត –
រាជាផ្ដា ឬ ក៏ជាកំប្រុកអេះ
ដែលខ្ញុំឯមើលនោះ?
មិនមែននេះ មិនមែននោះ អត់ទាំងអស់!

"ក្ដៅល្ម៉មែនទេ?" ស្ត្រីស្ដេងឡើង ។
"ពិតហើយ – គឺជា ស្ដ៊ឹង!" ខ្ញុំតបវិញ
យើងដើរឆ្ពោះផ្សារ ទន្ទឹមគ្នា ។
ការងារទូតជាកិរិយាខ្ញុំឲ្យគាត់ចាប់ចិត្ត ។

"អ្នកអាយុប៉ុន្មានហើយ ខ្ញុំសុំសួរបានទេ?"
"ខ្ញុំអាយុ ៥២ ឆ្នាំ" ខ្ញុំប្រាប់គាត់ ។ "ឯខ្ញុំ ៥៤ ។"
"អ្នកដូចជាមាំនៅឡើយ!" ខ្ញុំបញ្ចើច
"ខ្ញុំនៅក្មេងតើ ។" "អូ អស្ចារ្យ!"

O CAPTAIN! MY CAPTAIN! BE MY TALISMAN!

Thursday, April 29, 1993: the weather takes a turn—
it's a warm morning
by 10:00 A.M.
when I saunter down to Gilbert Street.

A woman bends over, peels off her sweater
and stuffs it into her shoulderbag.
It's impolite to stare at her derrière,
so I look at squirrels instead.

My senses swim—
is it flowers or squirrels
that I'm really looking at?
Nyther, neether, none of the above!

"It's very warm, isn't it?" she declares.
"Sure . . . it's Spring!" I respond.
Side by side, we're heading downtown.
Diplomacy is the act of letting her have my way.

"How old are you, may I ask?"
"I'm fifty-two," I tell her. "And I'm fifty-four."
"You look very strong!" I exclaim.
"I feel young too." "Oh, that's wonderful!"

យើងពាក់ព័ន្ធគ្នានូវការសំណេះសំណាល
អំពីភាសា – ខ្មែរ និង អេស្បៀរ៉ាន់តូ ។
ខ្ញុំចាប់និយាយ
"មេយស្រឡះល្អមែន ។"

គាត់និយាយជាអេស្បៀរ៉ាន់តូ
ពាក្យហើរផុតក្បេរខ្ញុំ ។
យើងចូរឈ្លោះ និង អាស័យដ្ឋានគ្នា:
"ដរលីន ។" "សាម ។" អ្នកជងរបងជាមួយ វិថី ព្រាន ។

174 |

ម៉ោង ៦ ល្ងាច ដេរតាមផ្លូវ ហ្គីលបៀត ម្ដងទ្យេត ។
ក្នុងដំណើរទៅថ្នាក់អង់គ្លេស ខ្ញុំទស្សយើញ:
"មនុស្សតិចថ្លានៅខ្ញាចសច្ចធមិណាស់
ឯមនុស្សខ្លាក៏ស្ងប់ខ្លៀមចំណេះវិជ្ជា ណាស់ដែរ ។"

ឱព្រះជាម្ចាស់ "សូមជ្រកក្រោមម្លប់បារមីព្រះអង្គហើយ!"
សូមប្រជាជនទឹកដីអង្គរបានរួចជាអ្នកជា!
"ហើយសូមស្មោះត្រង់នឹងព្រះរបស់យើង
មានភក្ដីភាពចំពោះមាតុភូមិរបស់ខ្ញុំ!"

សឡ្បវខ្ញុំព្រះអង្គមានឈ្មោះជាអ្នកក្បត់ជាតិ
ត្រង់ខ្ញុំព្រះអង្គនិយាយការពិត ។
ខ្ញុំព្រះអង្គសូមស្បែថដោយឯឡ្បារិកថាមែន
ខ្ញុំព្រះអង្គជាអ្នកក្បត់ពួកបិសាចមែន មិនមែនក្បត់ព្រះឡ្បើយ ។

បពិត្រព្រះជាម្ចាស់ បណ្ដោយឱ្យមិត្តនិងមារ
យើញទុលបង្គុំពាក់ មេបញ្ជាការទុលបង្គុំ
នៅជាប់ ក ទុលបង្គុំ ជាវត្ថុសក្ដិសិទ្ធិ
ជានិត្តរូបពិសដ្ឋន សេរីភាព – ប្រជាធិបតេយ្យ ជងចុះ ។

We're engaged in conversation
about language—Khmer versus Esperanto.
I begin by pronouncing "Megh Sralah Laah Nah"
(It's a fine day).

She says it in Esperanto—
the words float right by me.
We exchange our names and addresses:
"Darlene." "Sam."—neighbors on Brown Street

❧ ❧

6:00 P.M., walking down Gilbert again
on my way to ESL class, I'm thinking
"brutes are afraid of truth,
while the ignorant abhor knowledge."

O God, "shadowed beneath Thy hand,"
may the people of Angkor be free—
and "forever stand, true to our God,
true to our native land!"

Now I'm branded by devils as a traitor to my nation
on the grounds that I'm a truth teller.
And I solemnly swear, that, yes, I am
a traitor to the devils, but not to God.

Yes, God, let friends and foes alike
know that I will always wear O Captain! My Captain!
around my neck as a pendant, my talisman,
the sacred symbol of freedom and democracy!

ពរព្រះចន្ទ

ឆ្នាំស្រែក ម៉ែវ ម៉ែវ
ខ្ញុំ ម៉ែវតបឆ្នាំវិញ
ម៉ោង ដប់ យប់ទៅហើយ
រាត្រីស្ងាត់ឈឹង – សែនសុខសាន្ត ។

ក្រឡេកមើលតាមបង្អួច
ឃើញថាសមាស "ស" តាមចន្លោះស្លឹកឈើសុំបង្ហប
ខ្ញុំចិតភ្លើងចង្កៀង
ក្រែងខ្ញុំយល់សប្តិទេដឹង ។

អូ អញ្ជ នៅក្នុងសុបិនជម្រក
នៅ ប្រាន ស្ទឹត ក្រុង អាយ៉ូវ៉ា គេ
ខ្ញុំយក រ៉ឺនតា មកពាក់
ពិនិត្យថាស "ស" ម្ដងទៀត ។

រាៈនៅតែ "ស" ដដែល
ខ្ញុំដោះ រ៉ឺនតា ចេញ
សំឡឹងថាស "ស" អណ្ណែតឆ្ពាះខ្ញុំ
ខ្លួសឡេីងៗ ផុតចុងព្រឹក្សា ។

ខ្ញុំរកមើលឆ្នា –
ឆ្នាទៅបាត់
ប្រហែលរាមកប្រាប់ខ្ញុំថាៈ
"មើល ន៎! ព្រះចន្ទពេញវង់គេី!"

LUNAR ENCHANTMENT
for Virginia Black

A cat meows, and meows . . .
I meow back to the cat.
It's 10:00 P.M.
It's quiet and peaceful.

I look through the window;
I see a white disk through the foliage.
I switch off the light,
wondering if I'm dreaming.

Oh . . . I'm in my safe refuge
on Brown Street, Iowa City.
I put on my glasses,
observe again the white disk.

It's still white.
I take off the glasses,
gaze at the white disk floating toward me,
higher and higher above the trees.

I search for the cat—
the cat is gone.
Maybe he or she was telling me:
"Look, it's the full moon!"

កាលពីក្មេង ចាស់ៗតែង
បញ្ឆោតក្មេងៗឲ្យងើបមើលព្រះខែ
ហើយចាក់ក្រឡេក រួចឲ្យនិយាយ ៖ "លោកខែៗ
ឲ្យសុំបាយកកម្មួយដុំ ត្រីអាំងមួយ ម៉ា!"

យប់នេះខ្ញុំតែម្នាក់ឯង
កំសាន្តសោភ័ណភាពព្រះចន្ទពេញវង់
ចាស់ៗតែងប្រាប់ខ្ញុំថា៖ "ស្រមោលខ្មៅៗ
នៅលើខែគឺម្លប់ដើមពោធិ

178

ហើយនៅក្រោមម្លប់ពោធិមាន
យាយម្នាក់អង្គុយនៅ កំ
តាត់គ្បាញសូត្រ
សំរាប់ឲ្យយើងស្វែកពាក់ ។

ចន្ទគ្រាសគឺពេលរាហ៊ូមកប្រលែង
ជាមួយព្រះចន្ទ ហើយកាលណាខែច្រានចេញ
រាហ៊ូលេបខែ ។ បើធ្លាយតាមជំនឿ
គឺប្រផ្នូលអាក្រក់ ។ ស្រវល្ងបើខ្លាក់វិញ ។"

បច្ចុប្បន្ន មនុស្សជើរលើខែបានហើយ
ហើយគេគ្មានឃើញដើមពោធិសោះ
ហើយគេក៏ឥតឃើញយាយ ឃើញកីអីដែរ
ស្រមោលខ្មៅៗគឺជាស្រមោលភ្នំវិញទេ ។

ខ្ញុំនឹកអាណិតដូនតាខ្ញុំណាស់
ទោះលោកដឹងថារឿងមិនពិតក៏ដោយ
លោកនៅលើករឿងសង្ឃឹមនោះឲ្យចៅៗស្តាប់
សង្ឃឹមជាថ្ងៃមុខនគរនឹងសប្បាយរីសប្បាយ ។

In the old days, my elders
tickled children to look
at the moon and to beg: "Oh, beautiful moon,
may I have a clump of cold rice and a grilled fish!"

Tonight, I'm alone
enjoying the beauty of the full moon.
They used to tell me the shadows on the
face of the moon were a bodhi tree

and in its shade an old woman
was sitting at her loom
weaving silk cloth
for the people on earth.

An eclipse was when Reahou came to
make love to the moon, and when she spurned him
he swallowed her. A bad omen if she slips
between his ribs, full harvest if he vomits her up.

But now men have walked on the moon
and they've never found that bodhi tree,
nor the old woman, nor the loom.
Those shadows were made, it seems, by mountains.

I feel pity for my ancestors,
knowing that the story is not true.
But they gave their children hope
that someday we will be prosperous.

ហើយមានពាក្យពីព្រេងព្រឹទ្ធថា៖
"ខែរះឆ្លងផុរ
កូនកើតមុនឪ
ពរតាជើរលេង ។"

ពាក្យម្យ៉ាងទៀតថា៖
"ដល់ខែមួយចំហៀង
ឆ្វេងទិសពាយ័ព្យ
ស្រុកយើងមានភ័ព្វ មន្ត្រីហ្លួងវៀរ ។"

តាមចក្ខុវិស័យខ្ញុំ នៅងអាមេរិក
ព្រះចន្ទវិលវ្ញ្ញខ្លូនវាពីកើតទោលិច
ដល់កម្ពុជា ខែរះពីកើតដដែល –
ខ្ញុំច្បាស់ណាស់រឿងនេះ ។

ឱ ចន្ទ ពេញបូណ៌មី –
នាំពរបវរ –
ជូនកម្ពុជា!
ប្រក់ – ព្រាំ – មាតុភូមិ
សុខដុមរមនា
ភូត កម្ពុជា –
សន្តិ ពន្លឺ!

—ថ្ងៃទី ៤ ខែ មិថុនា ១៩៩៣

One old prophecy says, "The moon
arcs over the path of our lives. The son
was born before the father, and the grandson
carries the grandpa out to take a walk."

Another states, "When the sliver of a moon
points toward the northwest of Cambodia,
our country will become lucky. At that time
the titles of high-ranking officials will be changed."

In my field of vision, here in America,
the white moon floats from East to West,
but when it reaches Cambodia, it will be
on the eastern border again, I'm sure.

O, Full Moon, bring my best wishes to Cambodia!
Sprinkle holy water over Her,
Restore Her happiness!
Bathe her with your light of Peace!

—June 4, 1993

ហែលក្នុងទន្លេស្រណោះមាតុភូមិ

រថយន្តល្បឿនស្ទុងទាំជៈកំសាន្ត
និស្ស្យិតក្មេងៗ រីករាយសប្បាយ
មិនដែល គិតទេពីរឿងទឹកបាយ
ច្រៀងសើចក្លាកក្លាយ រីករាយចិន្ដា

តែខ្ញុំនឹកណាស់ នឹកមាតុភូមិ!

អង្គុយប្រកិត ស្ងិទ្ធជាងព្រលឹង
និយាយសម្ដឹងហួសពីស្នេហា
បកស្រាយទ្រឹស្ដី ទស្សនវិជ្ជា
សាសនា សារវន្ត កំណាព្យ កាព្យឃ្លោង

តែខ្ញុំនឹកណាស់ នឹកដើមឈ្នោតលៃ!

មាត់តែនិយាយដែស្ងាបអង្វែល
សាច់ស្រីពុំដែលប៉ះសែងសុរិយា
ហាច្បូយ ព្រីញ្រាច គ្លួចប៉ុងប្រាថ្នា
សុំការ កប់ ខ្លួនព្ធុនក្រោយសំពត់

ទោះចិត្តប្រាថ្នា វាសនាសម្រេច

រុក្ខជាតិ ថ្ងៃភ្លឺ គង់ផ្ទួបមហន្តរាយ
ខ្យាច់ ផង្ស ទាំងឡ្បាយ ក្លាយពាងចានឆ្ការ៉ាំង
អាត្មាខ្លួនឯយ ម្តេចប៉ុងប្រណាំង
ប្រឆាំង្គិ គតាំង ច្ប្បាំងនឹងកាមា

ទន្លេសាបអើយ – ខ្ញុំនឹកមាតុណាស់!

SWIMMING IN THE SEA OF NOSTALGIA
for April K. McAllister

I see that the college students are happy—
hunger never once enters their minds—
they sing and joke around with each other.

But I'm very homesick—I think of my Motherland!

Sitting side by side, we're closer than body and soul.
I adore her while we're chatting,
arguing about tenets of philosophies,
major religions, prosody, lyrics.

But I'm obsessed with the tallest sugar palm tree.

I pet her and pet her, while I continue to jabber;
she never exposes her skin to the sun's rays.
My heart throbs, craves, and wants to
ask for her hand so that I can hide behind her skirts.

Although this is my heart's desire, only fate can determine it.

Even trees, forests, mountains meet with disasters.
Even sand and clay can be transformed into jars, dishes, pots . . .
Why should I myself intend
to struggle against desire?

Tonle Sap, *oeuy,* how I long for thee!

ក្របី គោព្រៃ ជ័រ ទន្សោង
ខ្ញុំអស់ពេលឈោង ម្យ៉ងមើលទៀតហើយ
ពោធិ ក្ញោក ស្ពៅ ស្វាយធ្មាយផុតកោះត្រើយ
ឱរាលស្ពៅអើយ ទូលមួង – កំពង់ត្រាំ!

ឱ សែនស្រណោះ សម្ភស្សកម្ពុជា!

អង្គរវត្ត អើយ បាយ័ន បន្ទាយស្រី
តាព្រហ្ម បាទី ប្រាសាទព្រះវិហារ
ដែនសមុទ្ទ អើយ ដឹងទៅយ៉ាងណា
កោះ កោះ បានគេ ទន្ទេរក៏គោក

ហិនហោចអស់ហើយ ដោយ គំនិតឧក្ការ ។

ឱ បងផ្ញើ ម្ចាស់នៅទិណ្ណា!
សម្ងឹងរវហា ខ្យរលើសសមុទ្ទ
ពឹងលើវាសនា ចាប់ផុត ចាប់ផុត
ទុក្ខនេះអាលរាល ខ្លោចអស់បញ្ញា

ឱ រាលព្រែអើយ ព្រៃស្រូវមាតុភូមិ!

ខ្ញុំគ្មានបំណង ចរចាក ចេញទេ
ខ្ញុំស្ងេងរកព្រះ ប្រទេសកាមេ
ធ្លាក់ក្នុងទន្លេស្រណោះមាតុភូមិ
ហេលក្នុងទន្លេស្រណោះមាតុភូមិ ។

Oh, water buffaloes, bulls, horses, elephants, tonsongs—
the time will never come when I can gaze at them again!
Banyan, palm, neem and mango trees are beyond my vision!
Oh, prairies *oeuy*, Mound Muong, Kompong Tram!

How I miss the beauty of Cambodia!

Oh, Angkor Wat, Bayon, Banteay Srei!
Oh, Ta Prohm of Bati, the temple of Preah Vihea!
Cambodian Sea, *oeuy*, what will become of you!
Our islands go to the neighbors, while Tonle fills with silt.

They're all disintegrating because of power hunger!

Great-grandpa Raja, *oeuy*, Grandpas Suos and Jey,
Ta Euv, Gong of Victory, Hermit of Fire Eyes,
Daun Samrita, the Mother's Magic Veil—
all rain their blessings on Cambodia!

Oh, General Rang Sei, where are you?
I'm searching for you in the sky, but it's deeper than the ocean.
I count on destiny—everything is out of my reach.
Agonies scorch me, desiccate my intellect.

Oh, paddy field! The paddy fields of my Motherland!

I have no intention of abandoning you.
I'm seeking God, and I'm faced with Desire,
and I've fallen into the sea of nostalgia,
yes, I'm swimming in the sea of nostalgia.

ចំពោះយុវជន

យើញមេយស្រឡះ ខ្លាសណ្ណាស់ពេកណ្ណា
មានជាតិនឹងគេ តែជាតធូរចត់
ជនកម្ពុជា តែធំ សុទ្ធចាញ់សម្បូច
រាស្ត្ររស់កំសត់ ព្រាត់ប្រាសកូនចៅ ។

អ្នកស្នេហាជាតិ ស្នេហាតែមាត់
ឯចិត្តទេរទុត្ត មិនស្មាល់រាក់ជ្រៅ
ទស្សនវិជ្ជា ពុំចារទុកនៅ
ស្រែកដួចតាវៅ ចិត្តក្លៅដួចអគ្គី ។

បើបានធ្វើខុស មិនដែលតែប្រែ
ប្រឹងជេរល ស្រកជេរ បំផ្លាញសាមគ្គី
ឧបណ្ឌិតអើយ កុំចេះតែស្តី
សរសេរជាក្បួន បង្កើតទុកក្បៅ ។

បណ្ឌិត ប៉ាំង-ខាត់ បាត់តែជាតុប្បួ
ឯ ក្បួនគង់នៅ តម្រូវតម្រា
អ្នករ៉ាងគូច គូច គូរយកសិក្សា
ចំរើនបញ្ញា ស្ថារប្រទេសជាតិ ។

ស្រីហរិគោពទេស ឧត្តុឡ្ងឧត្តម
អ្នកនាងគូចខំ ទទេញ កុំឃ្យាត
ពិនិត្យ ក្អែក កុក អានហើយ អានឡេត
យល់ពិតទៅបជាតិ ឃ្យាតមហន្តរាយ ។

TO THE TEENAGERS
for Jesse Knute Smith

Now that the skies have cleared, I see that I have a nation
like everyone else, but the taste is bitter to my mouth.
Our countrymen in power now can't follow through on their word,
and citizens lead miserable lives, their families shattered.

They proclaim that they are patriots, but it's only words.
Their hearts are black, they don't understand politics at all,
and they never write their philosophies down on paper.
They croak like the raven, with a heart hotter than embers.

Whatever they've done wrong, they leave it just as it is.
Their way is to brag, belittle, and insult others, destroying unity.
Pundits, *oeuy*, don't just run off at the mouth—
You must formulate your ideas into monuments.

Pundit Pang Khat decomposed into the four elements
while his works remain as laws to be followed.
O, teenagers, you should take them into your minds
so that your intellects will one day blossom.

These Sreihitopates are most eminent.
O, teenagers, try to memorize every phrase—
and scrutinize the crow and the white egret; when you
understand their secrets, our nation will be beyond catastrophe.

កុំយកតម្រាប់កំពោងអាចម៍គោ
តែភ្លៀងធ្លាក់ឈ្នូរ អាចម៍គោ រលាយ
កំពោងអស់អាចម៍ បំបាំងរាងកាយ
ជួបក្តីអន្តរាយ រលាយរប្បធមិ ។

ដំឡូងអត់មើម មានប្រយោជន៍អី
មនុស្សមានតែសំជី ដូចស្រូវអត់គ្រាប់
ចំណោះផ្ជៅផ្ជះ ទើបទព្ទារាប់
គុណធមិ គួរគាប់ រាប់មនុស្សទេរា ។

Don't follow the example of the dung beetle,
for when the rain falls, the cow dung melts
and the beetle no longer has a place of shelter.
That way leads to catastrophe; the culture will crumble.

What good is a yam that can't send out runners?
The person with only words is like rice without a germ.
The Gods favor only those who have knowledge;
only virtue can bring people to mutual respect.

ទិន្នញធម្មជាតិនៅកម្ពុជា

ដើមត្នោតស្រែកថ្ងូរ ដើមពោធិ៍ស្រែកយំ
ព្រៃភ្នំស្រែកទទួញ រក អ្នកមានបុណ្យ
ទន្លេសាបសោតស្រែកក្រែងជាប់គុន
ព្រោះចាស់ជាន់មុន ជេរមាន់ទ្បៀតហើយ ។

ស្ដោៗនៅមិនសុខ ខ្លាចអភិវឌ្ឍន៍
សត្វព្រៃប្រាសប្រាត់ពិតពុំខានទ្បើយ
ជ្រាំជ្រាបធរណីក្ដិនស្អុយពិតហើយ
ឱមាតុភូមិអើយ មាតុភូមិកម្ពុជា ។

ត្រីរាជ ផ្ការ ឆ្នាំង ត្រីពោ ក្រពាត់
កំភ្លាញខាៗមាត់ ស្ងួញ ផ្នក់ វ៉ស់ ប្រា
អន្ទង់ កន្ធុប មុខបាត់គ្នា
អាសូរប្រជា ប្រជាជនខ្មែរ ។

ខ្មែរខំស៊ូ ដើម្បីសន្តិភាព
ដល់ពេលស្រុករាបអត់ដីធ្វើស្រែ
ដាកទៅរកត្រី អត់បឹងទន្លេ
កូនយំ ទ្បៀ ទ្បៀ "ម៉ែ! ម៉ែ! ហ្ាឃបាយញ៉ះ!"

បែរទៅរកឱស ត្រូវតែទិញគេ
បោះឆ្នោតពិសេម បានស្ងេច ជាម្ចាស់
ប្រឹងបំពេរក្ស ក្រែងបានកូនផ្ទះ
ដល់មេបក្សណ៉ះ ផ្ដះបានយួន – ចិន ។

THE MOANING NATURE OF CAMBODIA
for Carolyn Forché

The sugar palms moan; the banyan trees wail;
forests, mountains cry for an ideal leader;
the Great Lake trembles, fearing oil prospectors;
for the generation of roosters is back.

Neem trees are scared of rural development,
science, progress; wildlife will vanish for sure.
Sewage fouls the environment—no way out.
Oh, Cambodia, my beloved motherland!

Oh Fish King, carps, chhlang, po, krapeat! Little fish, stop bubbling,
chhlogn, ros, pra—
eels and frogs shall find no more water!
Oh, my lugubrious Khmer people!

Khmers struggled for peace, but when war ended
not a one found land on which to grow their rice.
They found no lakes or rivers in which to fish,
while children cried *lé, lé* for a clump of rice.

To cook, they even had to buy their firewood.
They elected a leader but got a caesar!
They served the Party, hoping to get a hut;
when the Party won, Viet and Chinese owned the houses.

រៀតណាមច្បាំងគ្នា ស្តេចខ្មែរក្បេរសខ្លួន
កែនខ្មែរផ្ទួយយួន សំលាប់ខ្មែរហិន
ខ្មែរសល់ពីជាប់ កំសត់ ខ្វាក់ ខ្ទិន
ប្រឹងបន់ព្រះគន្ធ វំដោះ ខ្លោះ ឃ្វាង ។

ព្រលឹងខ្មែរអើយ ផ្ទួយប្ដឹងទេព្តា
ពិតទូលផង្គា សុំពោធិសត្ត្វយាង
យោធយកកំណើត កើតជាមេជាង
កសាងយុត្តិធមិ លើដែនផ្ទាសា ។

When Vietnamese fought each other, the King
fled, appealing to Khmers to help the VC kill Khmers.
Fleeced survivors, blind and lame, prayed for God's help
to free each other from chains, shackles, and stocks.

May the souls of the slaughtered low together
plead that God assign us a Boddhisattva
to incarnate as the master architect
who will rebuild justice in our cursed land.

សុបិនក្រោយតែងសេចក្ដីអំពារនារសម្ដ្ឋកម្ពុជា
សិរិភាពនិងលទ្ធិប្រជាធិបតេយ្យ

ខ្ញុំហោលឆ្លងព្រៃកម្ពុយលើងលើ្យ
ឡើងជេីរកាត់ព្រៃ ស្រាប់តែជារ
ធ្លាក់ខ្លាកៗ ពីចុងលើ – ខ្ញុះទេីរលើរល្ង៉
ខ្ញុំជើសជារខ្ងះប្រុងយកទុកតាំង
ប៉ុន្ន្តែមេីលទៅមុខនៃបៗ ពណិ៍ក្រមៗៗ
"ពិតជាជារជើពុនចាក់ខ្មែរសម្ងាប់ហេីយ!"
"ជាជារឈាមស្រែក ស្ងៀកហោៗតេ!"
ខ្ញុំក៏បោះចោលវិញ

ក្រឡេកទៅមុខ – មានព្រៃកម្ពុយទ្យេត
ទុកចម្ងង ក៏ចេញផុតពីច្រាំងទៅទ្យេត
មានក្ងុងល្ងិតពីរនាក់រត់ផ្សែក
ហោៗទុកមកវិញ តែឆតប្រយោជន៍ ។

កម្ម្ងាះម្ងាក់ធ្លាក់ក្ងុងអណ្ដូងជ្រៅ
សុទ្ធតែភក់ខ្ងោចមាន់ល្ងៃយ
ពេលមាណាពលិចស្រ៊ីមទៅ
ខ្ញុំរត់ទៅចាប់សក់ទាញឡើីង –
ហ្ងសពេល ហ្ងសពេលហេីយ
កម្ម្ងាះលិចក្ងុងជ្រៅខ្ងោចមាន់បាត់ឈឺង!

DREAM AFTER COMPOSING THE APPEAL
OF THE CAMBODIAN LEAGUE
FOR FREEDOM AND DEMOCRACY

for Rose Rutherford

I am swimming across a wide river
when swords start falling from the trees
They must be swords left by the Japanese
I pick up several to save as collector's items
but the blades are rusty with deep nicks
They must have been used to butcher many Cambodians
whose tormented spirits may still inhabit the swords
I decide not to take souvenirs

And now I must cross another river
The ferry has just pulled away from the shore
Two little boys run after the ferry
calling it back for me to no avail

A young man falls in the quagmire of filth
the mud and hundreds of putrid chicken carcasses
As he sinks I rush to grasp his hair
too late. Too late. He disappears
in the foul mess as I just stand there . . .

បណ្ឌិត បីអង្គ ចង់ឈ្នះបារមី

ខ្មែរខំធ្វើបុណ្យ ថៃ-វៀត បានសុខ
ខ្មែរបានដេករៀន ថៃ – វៀត ដេកលើពូក

ខ្មែរសម្លាប់គ្នា វៀត-ថៃ ប្រមូលភោគ
ខ្មែរធ្វើស្រែលើគោក ថៃ-វៀតយកសមុទ្ទ ។

បីអង្គសុទ្ធបណ្ឌិត គិតមិនចេញ
ចង់តែចំណេញ មិនទិញបែរសំឡុត

សម្លាប់ខ្មែរចេះ ប្រហារខ្មែរស្ងួត
ទាញកម្ពុជាឲ្យទុគ៌ិត ព្រជាង ថៃ-វៀត ឡើងរុងរឿង ។

THE THREE WISE MEN WHO
WANT TO OUTDO GOD

Cambodians pray for blessings, but it's
the Thai and Vietnamese who enjoy peace.

Cambodians sleep all balled up on the ground,
Thai and Vietnamese sleep on mattresses.

Cambodians slaughter each other, while
Thai and Vietnamese pocket their wealth.

Cambodians try to grow rice in the highlands,
Thai and Vietnamese jostle for land near the sea.

Three wise men are struggling for power;
they get rich by raking in plunder.

They put to death the learned ones
and mistreat those who are honest.

They send Cambodia back to the Stone Age
and raise Thailand and Vietnam to glory.

សូមព្រះប្រជាធិបតេយ្យស្រង់កម្ពុជា

ទោះទន្លេធំភ្នំខ្ពស់   ចិត្តខ្ញុំមិនអស់
មិនហើយតស៊ូ   ចង់ឃើញកម្ពុជា
ផុតការបង្ហូរ   ឈាម បែរស្ដាប់ត្រ
                    ព្រះពុទ្ធគោត្តម ។

ការបង្ហូរឈាម   ផ្ទួបតែរហាម
ព្រោះការបង្ខំ   ជាចទហ៊ីង្សា
អ្នកចាញ់ទ្បញ្ញយំ   បែកសាច់ញ្ញាតិក្រុម
                    បាត់បង់សង្ឃារ ។

ប្រជាធិបតេយ្យ   បរថ្មាថ្ងៃ
គាំងពីបរមបរា   ព្រះពុទ្ធចែងច្បាស់
ក្នុងពុទ្ធសាសនា   ការឯកភាពគ្នា
                    ជាវិន័យសង្ឃ ។

ចុះកម្ពុជា   គ្រប់គ្នាជឹងថា
ជាជីពុទ្ធអង្គ   ទាំងប្រជាស្ដេច
គួរតែតម្រង់   ស្មារតីឲ្យត្រង់
                    តាមពុទ្ធដីកា ។

កុំអ្នកថា ខ្ទន   ជេីការន់មាមួន
ព្រះពុទ្ធសា៉សនា   បែរចិត្តទេវទត្ត
មាត់ជាទេវគា   សម្ឡាប់ប្រហារ
               ខ្មែរខ្ទ្រត់សូតគ្រង់ ។

MAY THE GOD DEMOCRACY RESURRECT CAMBODIA

A vast sea and many mountains separate me   yet my heart remains engaged
in the struggle,   for I want Cambodia
to stanch the flow of blood   and listen to our guru
         Gautama, the Buddha.

The killings   beget nothing but bereavement,
for oppression   is violence
causing the victims to lament   being torn from their kinfolk
         and the interminable loss of lives.

The theory of Democracy   is high-minded yet practical—
it's been around for ages;   the Buddha preached it
with great clarity: indivisibility
         is the discipline of the group.

And in Cambodia   everyone knows
they are under Buddha's sway;   hence, both commoner and king
should straighten   their minds to the truths
         of Buddha's Teachings.

How can we boast   that we all have faith
in Buddhism   if we display the heart of Devadatta
cloaked in the scriptures   while we maim and slaughter
         innocent and destitute Khmers?

វិញ្ញាណសត្តុណា					កើតក្នុងលោកា
មហាធាតុជាអង្គ					នៅវតម្មុជា
ត្រវប្រហារបង់					ទោះខ្ចូចទោះត្រង់
     គ្មានស្គាល់យុត្តិធម៌ ។

ពួជកាន់អាវុធ					តាំងខ្លួនបរិសុទ្ធ
ត្រុតប្រជាករ					តំរាម៉កំហែង
បង្ខ្ចិយកល្ល					ឲ្យរាស្ត្រកាំទ្រ
     អំពើជិះជាន់ ។

ឱជាតិខ្មែរឆ្លើយ					ពុំគួរសោះទ្បើយ
បាត់បង់ភូមិដ្ឋាន					ដោយពួជសាសន៍ថ្មី
បង្ខ្ចេងដើមជាន					ស្តេចភ្លេចវិញ្ញាណ
     ឈានចូលកងទុក្ខ ។

ប្រជាធិបតេយ្យ					ព្រះលើលោកិយ
ស្គាល់ទុក្ខដឹងសុខ					ទេិបឈ្មះអស់មារ
គ្រប់គ្រងភូមិស្រុក					ប្រជាឈានមុខ
     ការពារភូមិដ្ឋាន ។

ព្រះឆើយជួយខ្មែរ					មូលមិត្តុសាមគ្គី
ជួបញាតិសន្តាន					បានរស់ស្មើមុខ
ជួបសុខក្សេមក្សាន្ត					សូមខ្មែរគ្រប់ប្រាណ
     ឆ្ងងផុតរវាលបិ ។

The soul of any being   reincarnates into this world—
the predominant fate   in Cambodia
is getting murdered—   the blameless along with the traitors:
                    is there no justice?

The clique which has weapons   proclaims that they are honest;
they oppress their neighbors,   threaten them,
force them   to pay lip service
                    and to cave in to nepotism.

Oh, Cambodians, *oeuy!*   we shouldn't be
cut off from our land—   it's all because of the new race in power
who are conjure artists   who cause our king to lose his mind
                    and stumble into pitfalls.
                                                    | 201

If Democracy were to rule   as God of the world
she could discriminate between peace and pitfalls   then vanquish the enemies—
she would govern the country   by letting our people raise their voices
                    in her defense.

May this same God help Khmers   help Cambodians reunite;
let them rejoin their families,   let them live as equals,
let them live in peace,   let all Cambodians
                    cross over the three wildernesses.

កិច្ចការនៅខ្មៃគ្មាស ផ្តៃកចាក់ជ័រយ៉ូរីថេន

រាល់ថ្ងៃចន្ទ ដល់ ថ្ងៃព្រហស្បតិ៍
កិច្ចការចាប់ផ្តើម
នៅម៉ោង ៦ ព្រឹក
ហើយ ផ្សួហ្ស ជាអ្នករៀបចំកម្មវិធី ។

អក្សរផុសនៅកញ្ចក់កុំព្យូទ័រ ៖
ESCORT LX URETHANE PROGRAM
HIT THE START BUTTON TO
BEGIN THE POURING PART.

"ជាវេនឯងហើយ សាម!" ផ្សួហ្សស្រែកឡើង ។
ខ្ញុំលើកបន្ទះក្តារ ១ម៉ x ១ម៉ ឮូនជ្រុងពីរទេះ
ដាក់លើ តុ កង់
ចិទច្បាកឈ្មោះលើបន្ទះក្តារ

តម្រង់ច្បាកឈ្មោះ
ទៅនឹង អក្សរ និង លេខ ៖
A22 to A4
M22 to M4

ប្រធានរោងចក្រ និង អ្នកចាត់ការ
ជើរមកស្វាគមន៍ខ្ញុំរាល់ព្រឹក៖
"អរុណសួស្តី សាម
សប្បាយ សប្បាយ!"

"អរុណសួស្តី សប្បាយ សប្បាយ!"
ខ្ញុំឆ្លើយដោយមិនបាច់ងាកពីកិច្ចការ
ខ្ញុំញញបន្ទះក្តារចូលក្រោមម្ទូលបង្គរជ័រ
ចុចគន្លឹះសឲ្យយ៉ូរីថេនហូរលើច្បាកឈ្មោះ ។

WORK AT THE DOUGLAS CORPORATION, URETHANE DEPARTMENT, MINNEAPOLIS, MINNESOTA

for Ryan Skanse

At 6:00 A.M.
Monday through Thursday,
the work begins: Jeff adjusts
the urethane program.

It appears on the computer screen:
ESCORT LX URETHANE PROGRAM
HIT THE START BUTTON TO
BEGIN THE POURING PARTS.

"It's all yours, Sam!" Jeff shouts.
I lift the chase from the cart,
put it on the conveyor,
lay out the nameplates on the chase,

align the nameplates
to the alphabets and numbers:
A 22 to A 4
M 22 to M 4

Each morning the managers
and the president come to welcome us:
"Good morning, Sam!
Arun suor sdei, sabbay, sabbay!"

"Arun suor sdei, sabbay, sabbay!"
I respond without shifting my attention from my work.
I push the chase under the pouring parts,
hit the button to pour urethane on the nameplates.

កិច្ចការដែលៗប្រព្រឹត្តទៅពេញមួយថ្ងៃ
លើកលែងតែពេលសំរាក ១៥ នាទីនាម៉ោង ៩:៤៥
អាហារត្រង់ពីម៉ោង ១២:៣០ ដល់ ម៉ោង ១:០០ រជ្រ
ហើយសំរាក ១៥ នាទីឡ្យេតទៅម៉ោង ៣ រសៀល ។

ជ្យុន ប្រធានផ្នែកខ្ញុំ
ស្រែកម្លូង ម្ដាល:
"ត្រូវមែនទេ សាម?"
"មែនហើយ!" ខ្ញុំផ្លើយអត់ទាំងគិតផង ។

ជ្យុហ្វុបំពងសម្ដេងពីអ្វីមិនដឹង –
"វាធ្វើឲ្យអញក្អាតដល់ហើយ!"
"ប៉ – អ – អា" ជ្យុន លាន់មាត់ ។ គ្រានេះខ្ញុំធ្វើការ
ហើយធ្វើការផ្ដិតផ្ដង់ឲ្យទំនិញធ្លាញ់ចក្ ។

ខ្ញុំនឹងបង្វែរកម្ម៉ាំងខ្ញុំ
ខាងសេរីភាព និង ប្រជាធិបតេយ្យ
ឲ្យប្រក្ចាយជាផលិតកម្ម សង្ឃឹមថារដ្ឋាភិបាល
ប្រើប្រាសលុយពន្ធខ្ញុំសំរាប់ទប់ដល់នឹងអ្នកផះជាន់ ។

ហើយសម្ដេងបករបស់ប្រធានាធិបតី ឃ្លិនតុន
សូត្រកំណាព្យ រ៉ិលក៍ ហ្ជិតម៉ិន: "ហ្ស៊ូរទៅ ទន្ទេ!
ហ្ស៊ូរនឹងទឹកជំនន់ និង ស្រុក
ជាមួយទឹកនាចទៅ!" ខូរខ្វ័រក្នុងអារម្មណ៍ខ្ញុំ ។

តែប្រហែលជាខ្ញុំបញ្ឆោតខ្លួនខ្ញុំទេដឹង
តើខ្ញុំតាំងខ្លួនជាកសិករ កម្មករនោងចក្រសូវៀត
កាលឆ្នាំ ១៩៥០ ឬ? តើខ្ញុំដឹងថា
អ្នកណាទៅជាអ្នកផះជាន់ពិតនោះ?

The same routine continues all day,
except for a fifteen-minute break at 9:45 A.M.,
lunch from 12:30 to 1:00 P.M. and
another fifteen-minute break at 3:00 P.M.

John, my supervisor,
shouts from time to time:
"Isn't that right, Sam?"
"That's right!" I respond without thinking.

Jeff gibes away about something—
"It's really pissing me off!"
"Y-e-a-h . . . ," John mumbles. Meanwhile I work
and work to make products delicious to the eye.

I will transmute my energy
for freedom and democracy
into production, hoping they'll use
my taxes to stem the oppressors.

And the echo of President Clinton
quoting Walt Whitman: "Flow on, river!
Flow with the flood-tide, and ebb
with the ebb-tide!" rumbles in my mind.

But maybe I am just fooling myself.
Do I sound like a Soviet factory worker,
from the 1950s? Do I have any idea
who the oppressors are, in actuality?

បរមសុខពិត

កូនប្រុសខ្ញុំបាន អាយុអិនអេស យល់ព្រម
ឲ្យទៅជួបផ្ដុំប្រធានក្នុងទៅសហារដ្ឋហើយ
ដូចនេះខ្ញុំត្រូវទ្វេកម្លាំងធ្វើការរហូតយប់ជ្រៅៗ
យកប្រាក់បង់ថ្លៃលិខិតឆ្លងដែននិងរត់ការ ។

ថ្ងៃនេះ – ការងារចាប់ពីម៉ោង ៧ ព្រឹកដល់ ១០:៣០ យប់ –
សូមអរគុណ ជួន – ប៉ុណ្ណាហ្ស៊ីរ៉ា ជាពោធិសត្តម្នាក់
ដែលឲ្យខ្ញុំធ្វើការលើសម៉ោងយ៉ាងនេះ
ដើម្បីរំដោះកូនចេញពីនិមសង្កត់សង្កិន ។

"គូរិណា តើអាចជួនខ្ញុំទៅផ្ទះបានទេ?"
ខ្ញុំអង្វរ អ្នកស្រីប្រធាន ។
"ពិតណាស់ សាម! អត់បញ្ហាទេ សាម"
នាងឆ្លើយយ៉ាងរួសរាយ ។

ខ្ញុំបន្តការងារយ៉ាងបរមសុខ
ចាក់ជំរ យូរីថេន លើឆ្នុកសោ
បេះដូងខ្ញុំប្រណាំងនឹងសម្លេងម៉ាស៊ីន
ចាក់ជំរដែលរត់ទ្វេដង្ហើមខ្ញុំទៅឡ្បេត ។

"សុខសប្បាយជាទេ សាម?"
គូរិណា ដំរាបសួរខ្ញុំម្ដងម្កាល ។
"ល្អណាស់ ល្អណាស់!" ខ្ញុំឆ្លើយ
ដោយពុំដកភ្នែកចេញពីវត្ថុត្រូវចាក់ជំរលើផង ។

GENUINE BLISS

for Mag Dimond

My boy has been approved by the INS
to join his wife and son in the States.
So I double my strength to work until late at night
to pay for the passport and paperwork.

Today—work from 7:00 A.M. to 10:30 P.M.—
thanks to John Ponozzo, a kind of Boddhisattva
who allows me to work this much overtime
to liberate my boy from tyranny.

"Would you please give me a ride home, Corinna?"
I beseech my Lady Supervisor.
"Sure, Sam! No problem, Sam," she responds
with a ring of delight in her voice.

I continue to work blissfully,
pouring urethane on key tag products.
My heart races with the pouring sounds
of the machine, at twice my breath rate.

"How are you doing, Sam?"
Corinna greets me from time to time.
"Very good, very good!" I respond,
without taking my eyes off the urethaned products.

គិតដល់កំណាព្យ "ខ្ញុំអាមេរិកាកំពុងច្រៀង – "
"ម្នាក់ៗច្រៀងពីអ្វីជារបស់អ្នកឬនាង ហើយមិនរវល់ពីរបស់អ្នកដទៃ ។"
ខ្ញុំស្មើចជានិច្ចដល់ *Douglas Corporation*
ដែលផ្តល់ការងារឲ្យគ្រប់ស្រទាប់មនុស្ស ។

ខ្មែរ វៀតណាម ថៃ និង មិកសិកកិន
ធ្វើការជាមួយគ្នាដូចសម្ម កត្ូរ
ក្នុងកន្លែងដ៏បានតម្រៃ ញ៉ាំងអ្នកទាំងអស់គ្នា
ឲ្យស្រស់ដូចភ្លៀងប្រស់ស្ងោៗក្រៀម ។

ទោះបីទៅវេនថ្ងៃ កម្មករ-កម្មការិនី
មានបប្ូរមោត់បិតបើកមិនឈប់ឈរ
ពីព្រលឹមទល់ព្រលប់ ភាពចុះសម្រេងគ្នា
ដូច "ខ្ញុំអាមេរិកាកំពុងច្រៀង" សាយទូទៅមិនដាច់ ។

ក្រោយធ្វើការពេញមួយថ្ងៃមក ខ្ញុំហាក់
ដូចជាណរលើក្បាលទៅៗហើយ
តែបរមសុខពិតទ្រទ្រង់ការសង្ឃឹមថា
បានឃើញក្ូនមក្ុម "ខ្ញុំអាមេរិកាកំពុងច្រៀង" ជាប្រាកដ ។

សង្ឃឹមថាគាត់នឹងស្ងួងរកសុចិនពិតរបស់គាត់
ជាជាងរស់នៅ
ក្នុងរង្វង់ក្ុម្ុយនិស្តឈ្មើចិន ។
សង្ឃឹមថាគាត់នឹងស្ងួងបានបញ្ចាលើសខ្ញុំទៅៗទៀត ។

ពេលកំពុងញ៉ាំសន័រិច អាហារគ្រង់
ខ្ញុំនឹកអាណិតស្ងេចខ្មែរ
បិតាខ្មែររក្រហាមក្នុងកំឡ្ុងឆ្នាំ ៧០ នោះ
ខ្ញុំឆ្ងល់តើព្រះអង្គនឹងទៅៗកើតបានណាទៅជាតិក្រោយ ។

Thinking of the poem "I Hear America Singing—"
"Each singing what belongs to him or her and to none else—"
I'm continually amazed that the Douglas Corporation
offers work to those from every walk of life.

Cambodians, Vietnamese, Thais, and Mexicans
work side by side like vegetables stirred in a soup
here in this beneficent place, which enchants them all
like the rain resurrects parched grasses.

Even during the day shift, when almost
every worker's lips and tongue blab ceaselessly
from dawn to dusk, the harmony of
"I Hear America Singing" is all-pervasive.

After a day of work I feel
like standing on my head,
but genuine bliss sustains my hope
of seeing my boy in the chorus of "I Hear America Singing,"

that he will pursue his true dreams
rather than casting his lot
in the Communist Circle of Indochina,
that he will acquire more wisdom than I.

At lunchtime, while eating Oscar Meyer sandwiches,
I feel pity for the King of Cambodia,
the progenitor of the Khmer Rouge in the '70s—
I wonder what will become of him in his next incarnation.

ម៉ោង ១០:៣០ បានមកដល់
កូរិណា ក៏ជូនខ្ញុំទៅផ្ទះ
"ត្រាន់តែប្រាប់ផ្សេងចុះ សាម!"
"បើកតាមផ្សរ ១៦៩ រួចបត់តាម អូលសាកូពី!"

នាងបើកឡ្យានវៃងកាត់ភ្លើងក្រហម
ធ្វើពោះរ្យៀនខ្ញុំជើតជាប់ចុងលើតែម្ចុង
"កុំព្រួយ សាម ខ្ញុំធ្លាប់បើកទីក្រុងគេ!
អា យើងឆ្លងហ្សសស្ថានទៅហើយ!

កុំព្រួយ ខ្ញុំស្គាល់ទាំងអស់កន្លែងនេះ!"
ហ្សស ស្ថានបុ៉មីងគុន ទៅហើយ!
នាងបត់ឡ្យានវិលវិញ ។ ទៅតាមផ្សរហ្ញឹងឬ?
ហ្សស អត់ទោស សាម!"

"បានឃើញទេសភាពល្អៗដែរ!" ខ្ញុំបរិញ ។
"តើអ្នកណាមិនចង់ជិះឡ្យានអ្នកប្រធានបើក
ទៅលើលោកនេះ!"
ត្រានោះនាងបោះពួយទៅមុខតាម អូលសាកូពី យ៉ាងល្យៀន ។

"យើងបើកហ្សសផ្សរ និសចុត ទៅហើយ!" នាងលាន់មាត់
ពេលនាងបត់ យូ-ធ្យៀន ។ "អា ផ្សរសេសគេ!"
ហើយនាងបោះពួយតាមផ្សរគូចនឹ៊ងបត់ឡ្យាន
រាហ្សសប្រាំបុ៉កពី និសចុត អារវៃ សូហ្ស តែម្ចុង ។

"នេះវៃ៍ និសចុត – រាល់ពេលខ្ញុំទៅធនាគារ
ខ្ញុំបើកតាមផ្សរហ្ញឹងឯង!" នាងនិយាយប្រាប់ខ្ញុំ ។
ការទស្សនាកំសាន្ដលប់នេះជាមួយប្រធានស្រី
វិសាយភាពស្ដុកស្ដាញ្ឋងស្បាហាកម្មកាលពីថ្ងៃអស់ធេង ។

—ថ្ងៃអង្គារទី ១០ តុលា ១៩៩៥

10:30 finally arrives.
Corinna gives me a lift home.
"Just show me the way, Sam!"
"Go by way of 169 South, then Old Shakopee Road!"

She zooms her car through a red light,
leaving my stomach hanging in a nearby tree.
"Don't worry, Sam, I'm used to driving in the city!
Ah, we're crossing the bridge!

Don't worry. I know my way around here!"
Far beyond the Bloomington Ferry Bridge
she reverses direction. "Is this the way?
Gosh, I'm sorry, Sam!"

"It's good sightseeing, anyway!" I respond.
"Who in the world doesn't like to go
joyriding with his Lady Supervisor!"
Meanwhile she rockets ahead on Old Shakopee Road.

"We have passed Nesbitt already," she says
as she whips into a U-turn. "Ah, one way."
So she darts into a driveway to back up her car.
It's five blocks beyond Nesbitt Avenue South.

"Here's Nesbitt—every time I go to the bank
this is the way I go," she tells me.
This night sightseeing with my Lady Supervisor
dissolves all the industrial frustrations of the day!

—Tuesday, October 10, 1995

ទស្សនសង្គមពោធិសត្ត

ក្រុមពោធិសត្ត ស្មារតីមធ្យ័ត
ប្រយ័ត្នប្រយែង ប្រើបញ្ញាញាណ
ធ្វើលើជាក់ស្តែង គ្មានចិត្តបង្អែង
                    បង្អិលសត្តុណា ។

អ្នកក្រទុគ៌ិត ថ្ងង់ខ្លៅកំសត់
ខ្ចិលឆ្លងកំព្រា ក្រុមពោធិសត្ត
ចាត់ទុកស្មើគ្នា មានសិទ្ធិវាចា
                    គ្រវាស្មើងរស់ ។

មានសិទ្ធិសម្តែង ប្រឡងប្រជែង
ស្មើងជីវភាពខ្ពស់ ស្មើងសុកមង្គល
ស្មើងយកកេរ្តិ៍ឈ្មោះ ស្មើងរស់ជាមនុស្ស
                    ស្មើ ស្មើ ភាពគ្នា ។

ក្រុមពោធិសត្ត មិនថាតែមាត់
បង្កើតការងារ ជ្រោងផលិតកម្ម
បំបាត់វេទនា កសាងកម្ពុជា
                    នគរសេរី ។

ក្រុមពោធិសត្ត គោរពប្រតិបត្តិ
សីលធម៌ប្រពៃណី គោរពចាស់ទុំ
បំបាត់ឫកថៃ មនោ កាយ វចី
                    ឈរលើបញ្ចសីល ។

SOCIAL PHILOSOPHY
OF THE BODDHISATTVA GROUP

The Boddhisattva Group   dwells in conscious mind
acts with care, is scrupulous   uses the intellect
is realistic   avoids duplicity
       doesn't lead anyone astray.

The poor, the destitute   the deaf, the blind, the helpless
the disabled, the illiterate, the orphaned—   the Boddhisattva Group
regards them all as equals   who have the right to voice
       complaints about their daily lives.

They have the right to express themselves   to compete
to strive for a higher standard of living   to pursue happiness
to strive for a good name   to endeavor to live as human beings.
       The Boddhisattva Group extends these rights to everyone.

The Boddhisattva Group   doesn't just mouth these ideas
they create jobs   they increase production
they obliterate indigence   helping Cambodia evolve
       into a free land.

The Boddhisattva Group   obeys and practices
the old-fashioned customs of propriety: respect for elders
and shunning self-importance.   For them, mind, body, and speech
       stand on the Five Precepts.

ក្រុមពោធិសត្ត   គំកើងពលរដ្ឋ
បំបាត់ក្តីខ្ជិល   ទុក "ម៉ែជាធំ"
បំបាត់ខូចខិល   ជម្រះមន្ទិល
ជ្រោងទង់សាមគ្គី ។

ឆ្នាយបានមនុស្ស   ក្រុមពោធិសត្តទស្ស
ឈ្មេងគ្រប់ជីវី   នៃគ្រប់អង្គជាតិ
ថ្ម ស្វេ ឈ្មោលញី   វាល់ធួងថ្វាថ្ងៃ
សំណោញ្ជីវិត ។

The Boddhisattva Group empowers the people
banishes laziness gives mothers first consideration
obliterates deviousness and depravity erases suspicion
   hoists the flag of harmony over all.

The Boddhisattva Group pays this same respect
to all entities beyond the human realm:
the positive and negative— every strand is precious
    in the web of life.

Intda's Prophecy 1

THUNDER IN THE EAST: The Vietnam War against the U.S., from 1963 to its conclusion.

LOCAL ELDERS: The hierarchy of Buddhist monks who realized that they could do nothing about the impending spillover into Cambodia.

CRAYFISH: The Lon Nol group, including his brother Lon Non. Lon Nol ascended to the position of control of the country despite having no appropriate training or credentials.

WHITE EGRETS: The Viet Cong, waiting to attack.

BODHI TREE: Represents Buddhism in Cambodia, from 1960 to 1975. Both the Viet Cong and the Khmer Rouge were against Buddhism and often sent members to infiltrate the ranks of the ordained monks and spy for the Lon Nol group. One common tactic was to plant a weapon among the effects of a "problem" monk, and then "discover" it during a routine weapons search. The monk would, of course, be executed.

COBRA: This refers to Pol Pot, who hid out in the Roetana Kiri (the Mountain of Gems) and planned his move to power.

BUFFALO: The followers of Pol Pot. Buffalo commonly sharpen their horns by rubbing them against termite mounds in the jungle.

KING OF SWANS: A standard reference to Prince Sihanouk. This refers to his seeking political asylum in a number of countries before China, under Mao Tse-Tung and Chou En-Lai, welcomed him.

POPICH: A small brown fruit-eating bird about the size of a robin. No one seems to know which group this bird symbolizes.

BLACKCROWS, FIGS: Blackcrows symbolize the Khmer Rouge. Figs represent an attractive but deadly ideology (in this case, Communism). When the people look at the stored figs, they turn out to be rotten. It is implied that their former ideology (democracy) was better suited to their needs—they realize this after the fighting has stopped.

NUMBER OF FISH: The Viet Cong claim to know the number and the whereabouts of all the intellectuals.

GRAY EGRETS: Ill-bred louts of the Lon Nol regime. Gray egrets mark good fishing spots with piles of their own feces, returning to these same places; hence, they are easy to trap in that their movements are predictable.

SIEHA: The King of Lions, who is afraid of nothing. Refers to Prince Sihanouk.

DOMESTIC BULLS: The Hun Sen government.

TIGERS: The Khmer Rouge.

Intda's Prophecy 2

NOKOR KOK THLOK: The Khmer name for the Kingdom of Cambodia.

THREE STOCKS: Refers to the device in which one's head and hands are fastened for punishment and torture. The implication here is that the people of Cambodia are working to support three countries: Cambodia, Laos, and Vietnam.

GOSSIP AGAINST THEMSELVES: Refers to the Saturday afternoon autocriticism sessions under the Vietnamese regime, which were a continuation of a practice established under Pol Pot.

RAJA SIEHA: The King of Lions (refers to Prince Sihanouk).

TREE WITH THREE LADDERS: The tree is the Soviet Union, and the three bamboo ladders nailed into its bark are the governments of Cambodia, Laos, and Vietnam.

IN APRIL, THE RAIN: April is during the dry season, when such an occurrence is an impossibility. In the late '80s, the Phnom Penh government, backed by Vietnam, dug a canal across several provinces to the Vietnamese border. During the rainy season of 1991, a dam built during the Pol Pot regime eroded and broke because of increased flow from the canal. A five-mile long reservoir was released instantaneously, causing a flash flood which wiped out villages across three provinces. The flood reached Phnom Penh, sixty kilometers away. To gain international assistance, the government publicized this event as a natural disaster. They also suppressed the number of human lives lost, and much of the assistance wound up in the coffers of the middlemen.

SAMPOT: A wraparound skirt, similar to a sarong.

The Dispute for the Possession of Naga

RELATIVES TO THE NORTH: Laos.

GIANT TO THE EAST: Vietnam.

FULL SIBLING: Thailand.

DEVALOKAS: Angels, here symbolizing the non-Communist countries of Southeast Asia.

NAGA: The Pure One; the King of Snakes.

DEMONS: Symbolizes the Communist countries of the area.

MUONTARA MOUNTAIN: The Central Mountain, a mythical place.

SEA OF MILK: The world in general.

AMRITA: The nectar of bliss, the water of life, peace.

Oath of Allegiance

GAUTAMA: The Buddha's surname. Legend has it that the Buddha and his cousin Ananda once traveled through ancient Cambodia. The country was, at the time, uninhabited. The two of them stopped and sat in the shade of the thlok tree for their noon repast, which consisted of food from Heaven (i.e. food which materialized from the etheric plane). The thlok, incidentally, bears fruit which resembles that of the kiwi but has a big nut inside. During times of great privation, Cambodians have lived on this fruit. This is not, however, what the Buddha and his cousin were eating. As they ate, a large lizard (trakuot) came down the tree and begged for food. Since the lizard could not talk, it merely gestured toward the food with its forked tongue. The Buddha gave some of this magical food to the lizard and told his cousin that future inhabitants of this land would always have words which incorporate two aspects like the forked tongue of the lizard. For example, Cambodians say *moik duk-phuok*—*moik* is a verb meaning "to bathe" and *duk* means "water" while *phuok* means "mud." Hence, when Cambodians submerge themselves in a pond or river, they immerse themselves in water as well as mud, because the water is, by nature, murky. *Ptdah-sambeng* means "house," in general—*ptdah* is the main building while *sambeng* is a shack near the main house for sheltering cattle. *Slirk-beak* means "clothes," but *slirk* refers to garments which are pulled on from below, such as pants or skirts, and *beak* refers to garments which are worn on the upper body, such as shirts, bras, and blouses.

Bung Kriel

REAK: A children's game, similar to chess, which is played primarily by boys.

BIKOM: Another children's game, resembling jacks, played almost exclusively by girls.

Decision

SACHAM: "The Invisible People"—a group who are invisible but, otherwise, lead normal lives. They appear to right-minded people in times of need, often "adopting" a wayfarer for a significant period of time. But when the person returns to the "normal" world, it is as if no time has passed.

YOUR PESTLE IS MADE . . . : This comes from a traditional folktale about a ne'er-do-well farmer. The farmer works and works but never seems to make any headway. The only positive thing in his life is that he has a calico cat, an omen of good luck, but even the cat seems to have no influence in changing his misfortune. One night the farmer has a dream in which the cat appears to him and explains why he is faring so poorly—it is that his pestle is made of pong-ro wood (a very brittle kind of wood), his wife has only one breast, and his pond and well are situated unpropitiously. These are all considered to be signs of bad luck. The cat remarks that he cannot change the situation, as he is merely a cat. The farmer awakes the next morning and sees that his cat has spoken the truth. The story does not tell us what he decides to do.

Nightmare

BUDDHO!: My God!

DHARMO!: For the Lord's sake!

Prelude

TITH! HENG! PHON!: The names of the poet's neighbors.

ANGKAR: This term can refer to either the Khmer Rouge organization as a whole, or to any person in authority, from Pol Pot down to the village chief.

NHOM!: This is a term used by monks in referring to laypersons, meaning something like "aunt" or "uncle." The Khmer Rouge, in this instance, are asserting their feelings of superiority by using the term in a supercilious manner.

PHNOM PENH: Our house was located in Chbar Ampeou, a suburb of Phnom Penh. I wanted to go to Phnom Penh proper, where my brothers and their families lived.

Exodus

ORIENT WRISTWATCHES: A brand, made in Japan, having a status comparable to Rolex.

THEY STARTED TO EVACUATE PEOPLE: The population of Phnom Penh numbered 1.8 million. The evacuees were allowed to travel only along prescribed routes, which were so narrow that the people butted against each other, trampling the young, the sick, the elderly.

The Fall of Culture

PRECIOUS WEALTH: This refers specifically to both an Amrita crystal, which had no actual material value but was of inestimable spiritual value, and to volumes of poetry and philosophy.

NAGA FOUNTAIN WITH ITS SEVEN HEADS: A statue with seven hooded cobra heads.

MONUMENT OF INDEPENDENCE: A neoclassical monument built in Phnom Penh in 1957 to commemorate Cambodian independence from the French.

THOSE THREE WILDERNESSES: Wilderness of Killing, Wilderness of Starvation, Wilderness of Disease.

RANG TREES/THE SPAWNING GROUNDS: The rang tree grows on riverbanks; its roots grow out into the water and serve as a sheltered place for fish to lay their eggs.

POT-SARY CONFLAGRATION: Pol Pot, in cahoots with Ieng Sary, the Foreign Minister of Democratic Kampuchea, were the engineers of genocidal policies. Ieng Sary was the brother-in-law of Pol Pot.

The Loss of My Twins

TA: Colloquial for "Old Man"—used pejoratively.

THE TRIPLE GEM (OF BUDDHISM): Buddham (The Buddha), Dhammam (The Teachings), and Sangham (The Disciples).

My Invisible Sisters and Death by Execution

TA TRASAK PHEM: The Sweet Cucumber Dynasty, presided over by T. Jey, who became the king, Indravaraman III, in 1295.

SANGKUM: Society.

SAMDECH EUV: Refers to Prince Sihanouk. The literal meaning is "Prince-Father." In a 1967 speech, Prince Sihanouk said the following: "Kone chauv (my compatriots—literally, my children and grandchildren), you should not side with the Red (Communism). If my kone chauv wish to side with the Red, Samdech Euv must precede you—I can do that, for I am already intimate with their leaders.

But Euv will grant the rights to the Blue (free world and intellectuals) and the Red together to find peace for Cambodia. Wait and see how they are going to save our people. Kone chauv will see this come to pass."

INVISIBLE SISTERS: One invisible sister is Pido Mean Roeudhi, a princess from the Heavenly Realm, the other is the herb prateal, from Sharp Mountain, Kompong Speu.

PAGODITE: Soft mountain clay used for making statuary.

INVISIBLE SISTER: Here, referring to the leaves of the herb prateal.

Water Buffalo Cobra and the Prisoner of War

BUDDHA'S FLESH AND BLOOD: In a vision, I was told that whenever I came face-to-face with a poisonous snake I should recall Buddha, for Buddha was once born as a snake named Phuritatd.

SOUTH: Buddhist scripture says that teachers reside in the South.

The Elves Conceal My Buffalo and My Son

OEUY: An expletive of either loss or happiness, depending on the context—here it is loss, obviously.

PROELUNG: The phrase literally means "my soul." This was, at the time, my code name for my son. Every time we moved to a different camp I would give him a different name—this was part of our cover.

THEM: My son pointed to his invisible companions, the elves, with whom he had been playing and who had consequently rendered him invisible to me, even though, in reality, he had been right there in front of me earlier in the afternoon.

OLD PEOPLE: The Pol Pot clique and their sympathizers.

EVIDENCE: First, I had lost a water buffalo entrusted to me and then discovered that she had eaten a larger area of rice shoots.

FIRST DECENT MEAL: This was, in essence, a kind of "last supper" our overseers provided for people before they executed them.

SHORTHORNS APPEARS: She, too, had been hidden by the elves. I suspect that she had been nearby all the time but was being ridden by an elf and, was, therefore, invisible.

Dream at Phtdowl Concentration Camp

SAMOHAPHEAB: The term for the entire group, whether it be three people or twelve.

Season of Transplanting Rice

RED EYES: It is rumored that there was a practice among the Khmer Rouge of sneaking up behind young virgin girls, killing them with axes, then removing their livers and eating the livers raw. They believed that this gave them immortality. It also turned the whites of their eyes permanently yellow. On occasion, in past times as well as present, people have been known to eat the livers of enemies they have killed—I have heard of this on all the continents. I have also had people confess to me that they did this in wartime. To this day, I can spot someone who has done this by the color of his eyes.

Sacred Vows

VESVORN: King of Angels of the First Realm, assigned to look after the well-being of people in the northern part of the country.

"NAMO . . . SAMBUDDHASSA": Praise be to Him, the Blessed One, the Fully Enlightened One.

The Wheel Turns

YUON: Colloquial term for Vietnamese people—used pejoratively.

STIENGS AND PHNONGS: Ethnic minorities in the northeast jungles, especially Kracheh province.

KRAMA: Traditional checkered scarf, used for many purposes.

PHNOM CHI: The Fertilizing Mountain—initially I had believed that the Fertilizing Mountain was a place at which the Pol Pot clique had an operation in which they made fertilizer from animal and possibly human excrement. Since I had been assigned to do this for some time, it was logical, I thought, that they would be "transferring" me to that location. After we were liberated, some of us heard a widely circulated rumor that the Pol Pot clique had a motorized guillotine at the Fertilizing Moun-tain, and that they were beheading prisoners and rendering their remains into fertilizer, which they were sending to China. This is where they were herding us when the Vietnamese troops intercepted our group a few miles before we reached our grisly destination. Whether such an operation existed has never been substantiated.

"DENY HER . . . WOMAN": In 1973, an abbot (and fortune-teller) warned me, "You are not a talented orator; hence, you, personally, cannot do anything about the plight of the country. Don't befriend (take into your confidence) any woman other than your wife. Also, don't listen to any man who promises you rank or favors." This seemed very vague at the time, but I remembered what he said.

NEEM LEAVES: Leaves of the neem tree, used to treat fever. The taste is bitter, resembling quinine.

PREAH INDRA KOSEI: The King of Angels.

PIDO MEAN ROEUDHI: The Overwhelming Fragrance. (See note for "My Invisible Sisters and Death by Execution.")

PRINCESS LOTUS BUD: Princess Krabum Chhouk, the Unopened Lotus Bud.

MACHAH BONG: Elder princess.

Disorientation

"CO COEUM KHONG? TOI SIN COEUM MA CHUCK?": (said in Vietnamese) Do you have rice? May I have a little rice? That I answered him first in Vietnamese and then in English would normally have been grounds for the soldier to shoot me, this being an indication that I was an intellectual, but in this instance he merely gave me a hard look and allowed me to go forward.

TOCH THE ELF: From 1970-1979 all the deities were absent from Cambodia, having fled to places such as the Himalayas. Only demons remained. There were still elves around, however, because they were able to stand up to the demons on their own terms. I learned later that this particular elf, Toch, had been assigned to me as a guardian.

GRANDPA ANG PHIM: A spirit ordered by Grandpa Suos to protect me.

NEAKTA: The spirits in that particular place.

MY SON'S HOUSE: The house where my son was born.

The Krasang Tree at Prek Po

KRASANG: A tree which has long thorns on its bark and bears a sour nut-like fruit which villagers frequently add to soups.

PREK PO: A village fifty kilometers north of Phnom Penh.

UTAPATS: General term used to refer to evildoers.

Visitation

DEVINDA: The King of Angels.

EMERALD TEMPLE: A temple within the Royal Palace in Phnom Penh which contains a gold statue of Buddha and another Buddha carved from an emerald. It is widely believed that the Vietnamese took the two statues and substituted fakes, and that the originals are now cached in Hanoi.

HIS LIVER, HIS MARROW: My son had been bitten by a poisonous snake in 1970 and, in 1984, had become gravely ill. Devinda was telling me that my son's illness was the direct result of my carelessness in 1970, which had finally taken its toll.

DHORNVANTREI: Doctor sent by God to heal an individual designated by God as someone appropriate to be healed.

PREPARATIONS: This particular medicine was prepared from pollen collected by 120 virgins between the ages of twelve and thirteen. They would spread the pollen in the palms of their hands at night and let it mingle with the dew; hence, the unusually long time it took for this mixture to dry.

Humor at the Meeting to Strengthen Phum Khum

TRAKUON: a hardy creeping plant indigenous to Cambodia, of which some species are terrestrial, some aquatic. It is sometimes known as bindweed, sometimes as water morning glory. It grows rapidly and can be harvested every fifteen days. It is edible but was considered fit only for peasants prior to the Pol Pot regime. It became a symbol of the Vietnamese occupation in that Vietnamese troops devoured most of the trakuon in the countryside and would not allow Cambodians to forage for it, restricting them to eating what they, the Vietnamese, had provided.

The Angel Performs a Heavenly Dance

NAGARAJA'S PEARL: This refers to a pearl brought to me by Pido Mean Roeudhi, my invisible sister from the Heavenly Realm. She had been searching for me for forty years to no avail. One night she fell asleep exhausted in a cave, and when she woke up she realized that she had been sleeping in the mouth of Nagaraja (the

King of Snakes). He is both my spiritual father and hers. He gave her the pearl to bring to me for my protection. This was in the summer of 1972. She was told that when she reached the four affluents of the Mekong and found the royal palace at the village of Niroddha on the southeast bank, she would find me there, waiting in a bamboo thicket. This came to pass just as he had told her. When she met me there, she wept for joy, having searched for me for so long. I carried this pearl with me for several years but lost it in traveling from one concentration camp to another. My invisible relatives gave me another pearl, but this time they embedded it in my thigh so that I wouldn't lose it as easily.

Neo–Pol Pot

KOK THLOK: The name for Cambodia in the Khmer language.

BI-KOK: The cold cooked rice at the bottom of the pot remaining from the previous evening or noon meal.

KO-5: A battlefield at the Cambodian-Thai border. The People's Republic of Kampuchea mobilized young and old alike to participate in clearing the forests along the border from 1983 to 1989. The puppets told us, "It is the highest sacrifice to go to KO-5."

KAMPALM: Sour juice on the sugar palm tree. Anyone who drinks it gets drunk.

I Try to Survive for My Nation

Grandpa Kleang Moeung: Sixteenth-century warrior who was chief of the sub-district of Kravagn Mountain, Pursat. He gave his life to save the nation by helping the king fight against marauding warlords.

Grandpa Dek: Sixteenth-century nobleman. His faithful fiancée died from grief because she loved Grandpa Dek so deeply and her parents would not allow her to marry him. Her grave became a termite mound. People worship her spirit in order to have their wishes come true and, especially, to get their stolen cattle back. The story has it that one night her spirit came to tell Grandpa Dek that in the morning an elephant owned by the king was going to pass in front of the altar erected in her memory, and that it would fall dead. She told him, "You shouldn't save the elephant—if you do, you will die." But Grandpa Dek had taken vows to serve his people and the Triple Gem. He knew that, without the elephant, the king would have a poorer chance of defending his people and his country; accordingly, he saved the elephant, exchanging his own life in the process.

Mad Scene

"OUT FROM THE GLOOMY PAST . . ." : quoted from "Lift Ev'ry Voice and Sing," by James Weldon Johnson and J. Rosamond Johnson.

SAMDECH EUV!: Prince-Father (Khmer). I invoked the name of Sihanouk in hopes that he would restore peace and independence and grant human rights, freedom, and democracy to our people.

A Freshening Wind Is Rising

SEATO: Southeast Asia Treaty Organization, which included Cambodia's neighbors Malaysia, Indonesia, and Thailand.

TA KHMAO: Black Grandpa—the nickname for Lon Nol, prime minister at that time and later president of the Khmer Republic. He believed in oracles and prophecies, and sent a hastily gathered and totally untrained army against the Viet Cong. They were all killed.

FANK: The acronym for Lon Nol's army—Forces Armées Nationales Khmeres.

FUNK: The acronym for Prince Sihanouk's army—Front Uni National du Kampuchea.

ATHEISTS: Pol Pot clique, or Khmer Rouge.

ALIENS: Vietnamese troops, from 1979 to 1989.

YEAR OF THE GOAT: 1979.

GIANT: Vietnam.

ANCIENT ENEMY: Thailand.

YEAR OF THE DOG: 1982. **BOAR:** 1983. **TIGER:** 1984. **RABBIT:** 1985. **COBRA:** 1986. **GOAT:** 1987.

IF . . . EVERYWHERE: An ancient prophecy.

A5: A battlefield on the Thai-Cambodian border, 800 kilometers from Koh Kong province to the Triangle Frontier (the Laos-Cambodia-Thailand common border). Cambodians were mobilized (men, women, and youths) to clear the forests, to help prevent the Khmer Rouge from infiltrating the country by destroying their cover. The casualties in this campaign were staggering.

CHANSI: The prime minister at the time of A5. He spoke out against the mobilization on both moral and practical grounds—morally, because he said the cause was not just and, practically, because it took too many people away from their real work, which was agriculture. He was sent, by the Vietnamese, to the hospital in Hanoi to recuperate from "overwork," but while there, he suffered, according to the Vietnamese, a massive hemorrhage and died. He had a public funeral north of the Royal Palace in Phnom Penh, at which his body was cremated and Vietnamese officials mocked him openly.

DONG CHI: Comrade (Vietnamese).

YEAR OF THE DOG: 1994.

YEAR OF THE RAT: 1995.

HEAVEN ON EARTH: There are three levels of consciousness, according to Cambodian Buddhism—Manuh Peto, in which humans exist in a kind of purgatory; Manuh Terechhano, in which people exist on the level of beasts, often symbolized by the tiger, crocodile, white egret, and black crow; and Manuh Devo, in which all corruption has been eliminated and people coexist peacefully and have great understanding and compassion for each other.

The Ruins of Angkor Cry Out for National Concord

THE TEMPLE OF BAYON: North of Angkor Wat, but still part of Angkor City. It was built circa A.D. 1200 Angkor Wat was built A.D. 1113-1150.

BANTEAY SREI: The Woman's Fortress—a monument in the eastern part of Angkor City, built to honor the women warriors who fought to protect the city from the invaders from Siam. It was built slightly later than Bayon.

NAMKOC: Vietnam.

PATCHED CLOTHES: Indochinese Communists. Some women, of very questionable reputation, have become trade union presidents and ministers of industries.

HOE: Refers to Siam (Thailand), which has always tried to gain territory from Cambodia, as if chopping away at the land with a hoe.

KRAM NGOY: A Cambodian poet, 1865-1936. "Kram" is the title given to a political official who is a member of a subdistrict committee. It means, literally, "code of ethics." He used his title as his first name.

O Captain! My Captain! Be My Talisman!

"SHADOWED BENEATH . . . NATIVE LAND:" From "Lift Ev'ry Voice and Sing," by James Weldon Johnson and J. Rosamond Johnson.

NOW I'M BRANDED . . . TRUTH TELLER: In the early days of 1993 I received insulting letters from California which included death threats.

Lunar Enchantment

REAHOU: A giant who, in playing with the magic wheel of Vishnu, in order to obtain amrit (the nectar of bliss), was cut in half. The upper half of his body continued to function independently, while the lower half remained inert.

"THE SON . . . WALK": The interpretation of this is that the son is Prince Sihanouk, who was enthroned by the French in 1941. When the country gained independence in 1954, he abdicated and gave the throne to his father, Suraemaroeddhi. Sihanouk is often called Prince Norodom Sihanouk, and Norodom is the name of his grandfather; hence, he carries the name with him on public occasions.

"WHEN . . . CHANGED": This is a very old prophecy, and in October of 1987, the moon finally tilted to this particular angle. At that time the government discontinued the requirement of having everyone refer to each other as "comrade." Ironically, most officers began referring to themselves and having others refer to them as "excellency."

Swimming in the Sea of Nostalgia

TONLE SAP: The Great Lake of Cambodia, near Angkor Wat.

TONSONGS: A species of wild jungle cattle.

MOUND MUONG: A mound in Svey Rieng around which I used to herd cattle when I was a youth. The mound no longer exists.

KOMPONG TRAM: An area west of Phnom Penh, filled with sugar palms, where many people used to go on outings.

TA PROHM OF BATI: A temple built before the middle of the sixth century by Rudravarman, thirty kilometers south of Phnom Penh. Only the walls are left standing.

PREAH VIHEA: A temple perched atop a cliff in the highlands at the Thai border (Oudor Mean Chey province), which is now under the control of the Tourist Bureau of Thailand. Construction on the temple was begun in A.D. 893.

GONG OF VICTORY: A gong which has a distinct sound, which many have heard but few have actually seen, as it is from the Invisible Realm.

HERMIT OF FIRE EYES: Father of both Grandpas Suos and Jey.

GENERAL RANG SEI: The hero of the epic poem "Decjo Damdin." Son of a farmer, he became a general and was the only leader to defend the Khmer Empire during the Angkor era. He also liberated China from the Mongols and reunited the country. He was transformed into stone by the Magic Mouth.

To the Teenagers

SREIHITOPATES: Pang Khat's translation of Vishnu's "Free Good Counsel."

CROW: Khmer Rouge.

WHITE EGRET: Vietnamese.

The Moaning Nature of Cambodia

CHHLANG: A variety of river catfish. The largest fish in Cambodia, it is found only in the deepest parts of the Mekong, in Stung Treng province, bordering Laos.

PO: A larger variety of carp with black scales.

KRAPEAT: A slender, scaleless fish, two meters in length, with a dorsal fin running the length of its body.

CHHLOGN: A small fish, about the size of a smelt, which lives in river mud and in rice paddies.

ROS: A carp with white scales.

PRA: A catfish with a particularly large head.

The Three Wise Men Who Want to Outdo God

Even though the United States tried to reconcile the three Cambodian factions by conducting a free election in May of 1993, the leaders have continued to fight each other.

May the God Democracy Resurrect Cambodia

DEVADATTA: The cousin of Gautama, he was jealous of Gautama's reputation, even though he himself was quite charismatic. He realized that he could not get the better of Gautama in a one-on-one situation, so he declaimed against Gautama, saying that his eating of the flesh of animals was unenlightened and that his wearing of clothes was an indication that he lived in shame. Devadatta gathered a large group of disciples about him and they lived in the forests as vegetarians dressed in rags. Sariputra, another cousin of Gautama, disagreed with Devadatta's stance. He tracked him down in his stronghold, where Devadatta greeted him enthusiastically, assuming that Sariputra had come to join his ranks. Sariputra played along with this. Devadatta assigned him the task of ministering to his disciples while he (Devadatta) got some well-deserved sleep. While Devadatta slept, Sariputra defamed him so convincingly that all the disciples left the stronghold. When Devadatta awoke and found that all his disciples had abandoned him, he fell into a fit of rage so vehement that his circulatory system literally exploded and he died instantaneously.